"Angelo is a well-connected professional who always takes the time to support anyone is his network. Angelo did an exceptional job on recent projects, mainly using LinkedIn as a tool to connect professionals. Thank you, Angelo, for your efforts on connecting professionals around the globe." – **Robson Cazanato Galvao**, National Sales Manager at *Vibac Group* S.p.a., Brazil

"Angelo is a highly-motivated individual with very good communication skills and an exceptional eye for details. It was a pleasure to work with him, and I look forward to working with him again." – **Mike Anderson**, Account Executive at *Thermo-Rite*

"Angelo has provided me with vast knowledge. Angelo is a solid individual who has the candidates' and clients' best interests at heart. He has an excellent record of connecting with our best candidates. He truly cares about the success of everyone." – **Lorene Salomone**, Motivational Speaker

"Angelo is a very successful individual who enjoys what he does immensely. I had very pleasant interactions with him several times, and I heard many good comments about him from many other workers. He not only genuinely cares about his work but also possesses very good management and interaction skills. He is a very diligent and self-assured professional with whom everyone would enjoy working. I strongly recommend working with him to everyone without any doubt." – **Ayca Ertekin**, Advanced Technology Leader at *Greene, Tweed*

"Angelo's an extremely bright individual with a strong work ethic. It has been a pleasure working with Angelo over the years, as I can always count on him to follow through. He's straightforward and honest with the highest degree of integrity. He also brings tremendous value to his clients, as he is an expert in his space." **- John Moon**, Director of Talent at Precision Cast Products Corp., *Forged Products*

"Simply put, when I needed a job, Angelo was there to close the deal with a relevant job at a growing company and even commutable. He is my first call." **- Karen Capik-Berman**, Technical Manager at *Huhtamaki Films Inc.*

"Great book to guide you thru the job search process, the smart way." **- Uchralmaa Tumurbaatar**, Program Coordinator, *Cleveland State University*

YOU GOT THE JOB!

Turn Your Career Dreams into Reality

Published in the United States by Todaro Publishing, Cleveland, Ohio, 2017.

Library of Congress Cataloging in Publication Data
Giallombardo, Angelo
ISBN-13: 978-1543148053
Printed in the United States of America.

Cover Design By Zoran Kochoski
Author Photograph by Margaret Valletta
First Edition

Dedication

I'm dedicating this book to my mother Renee, my father Gary, my Grandpa Angelo, and my Grandpa Sam Todaro who have guided me, inspired me, and molded me into the man I've become today. Without the gift of their endless patience, attention, and guidance, none of this would be possible.

To my daughter Sylvena, you inspire me to be the best I can be every day of my life. Your smile strengthens my drive to achieve my dreams. May you reach for the stars, grab them one by one, and never look behind you.

To my ancestors who endured incredible hardships in order for my family and me to have the freedom to create the best possible life for ourselves, I feel I owe my existence and the time I spend on earth to you and your sacrifices.

To my friends and loved ones, including Victoria Avi, Daniel Hawrylak, Jesse Kanner, Rene Duffee, Doughboy Langley, Ken Janik, Courtney Winn, Dan Farina, John Moon, Steve Ozan, Tony Coppola, Ande Schewe, Chrissy Basile, Amy Marcus, Alex Hanlin, and Chris Heino. Without your support, none of this would be possible.

To my dear friends and family departed, including Faye Todaro, Mary Giallombardo, Grace Eggett, Colin McKnight,

Doug, Jack III, Jen Deniro, BJ Sommers, and Aunt Mary Russo. May you rest in peace forever.

To the thousands of job candidates I've had the pleasure of successfully serving, and especially to the ones I could not help, you've provided the experiences to help me write this book. Thank you!

Contents

Introduction

I'm super excited to be presenting this groundbreaking book and program to help you acquire your dream job. First and foremost, let me explain why this will be the best first step in your decision to find and acquire your dream job.

A little about me—I'm an Executive Recruiter and VP of Sales with Central Executive Search, Inc. where I've spent more than the last fifteen years providing value-added experience to candidates and clients in the manufacturing, polymer, chemical, and packaging-related manufacturing markets. My in-depth knowledge and firsthand experience working directly with job seekers and candidates at all levels of experience will direct and guide you through a proven step-by-step system by which you can land the job of your dreams.

Every day for over fifteen years, candidates have called and emailed me, asking me to help them find their next career advancement opportunity. Each time I connect with these everyday, hardworking folks, I try to help them understand what it will to take for them to land the position they want. I find that my advice, knowledge, and direct experience in these markets adds value to their job search and their lives. I also realize I can't realistically make enough time to help each and every person who contacts me via phone, email, or video conference.

My goal in my career is simple: I want to help people find that next advancement in their career. I'm here to help you learn how to put food on your family's table, secure enough money to pay your bills, pay for your daughter or son's college tuition, and earn the necessary compensation to help you achieve these goals, day to day, month to month. The real challenge in all of this is that I don't have the time to show every single one of you the step-by-step proven process to get your dream job. Because of the massive volume of candidates reaching out to me every day, there just isn't enough time in the day to consult with each of you and show you what it takes.

That's where this program comes into play. This book and program will be a comprehensive and complete showcase through which I can work with each and every one of you to help you land your dream job. This book can add extreme value to your job search and everyday life *if* you take it seriously and follow the advice presented. It will help you immensely because I see the pitfalls that most job seekers fall into in their job searches.

Because of my experience in these markets and my knowledge of how job seekers, the hiring manager, and interview teams think, act, and respond, the information I bring to you here will be invaluable to you and your search.

I've had many challenges in my career, and I choose to focus on how those challenges have made me stronger and fortified the real level of success I've accomplished. Without those challenges, I would not have been able to grow into my success. Almost all of the success I've had in my career is self-made. I've been able to place thousands of people in new careers and new job opportunities. For the last seven years, I've consistently grown my sales numbers each year while helping to place more and more people in jobs in which they are happy. In the last two years, I've broken records in sales that have been in place for over thirty years and have generated revenue for our company. Although I'm proud of some of these numbers-based accomplishments, the accomplishment I'm most proud of is helping everyday people and their families to find the career they desire. I've come to realize that helping people is my calling, and I've begun to see how amazing it can feel when what I do has a true impact, not just on the worker, but also on the person's family and their quality of living. Having a more purposeful career and making more money is something all of us want to do, and I'm blessed to be able to help people do just that every day.

The biggest reason I wrote this book was a deep feeling I had that I wanted to reach **more** people. I knew that if I wanted to reach more people and help them with my experience and knowledge, I had to write a book. People are what make the world a better place, and my contribution to humanity and everyday working people is what I feel is the most valuable thing I can do. In helping others, I know I've bettered the world and left a legacy of helping others to accomplish their dreams, goals, and aspirations. There are many ways to do this, but *my* gift is giving back to people through experience in job placement so they can better their lives. I am grateful to be able to give this gift to others.

I am very thankful to the job seekers I've worked with and for the experiences I've had over the course of my career that have helped shape my perspective so that I can help *you*. Again, I'm thrilled to bring this content to you, and I can't wait to teach you how to find the position that has been in your heart, your mind, and your dreams.

Chapter 1

The Phoenix Rises from the Ashes

"Choose a job you love, and you will never have to work a day in your life."
– Confucius

So why are you here? What circumstances have brought you? Is it your desire to find happiness and reach your full potential? Have you thought about the reasons that prompted you to gain more knowledge about a new opportunity? Do you have the necessary mindset to acquire the job of your dreams?

At some point, we all go through the process of trying to determine our path in life. We all have our place and purpose in life, and a job is really a path to finding ourselves and reaching our full, unique, and true potential. The fact that you're reading this book is validation enough that you truly want to find the path that leads to the career you've always wanted. True human potential is up to the career path seeker, ourselves.

I'm the guide, the compass, the conduit for your success. I'm happy to lead the way with my experience in helping people, step by step, to find their ideal job. Somehow, I found myself here as well, and it wasn't by accident. It was through hard decisions, a lot of soul searching, digging deep and uncovering truths, and yearning for fulfillment through my calling to help others. That's all I ever wanted to do.

As a kid and adolescent, much like many of you, I thought I had it all figured out. I just *knew* I was going to help others. I studied my passions, graduated with a degree in plant biology, and thought I was destined to teach and be a part of the natural healing and plant medicines markets. One of the main reasons I studied in that area was because I was diagnosed with Crohn's disease at the early age of twelve. For those of you who don't know, Crohn's disease is a genetic autoimmune disease that affects the digestive tract. Stress is a major trigger for the disease, and I suffered with it throughout high school and college. Thankfully, I made it through college, but the sharp pain came often and was persistent. I spent many days in debilitating pain.

Little did I know that after graduating, I would find myself out of work and then in a job where no one seemed to care about my perspective and point of view. Only then did I get the break, the opportunity I should have seen from the start.

You see, after college, I was broke. I had lost all of my possessions in a storage area that got swamped in sewage. Everything I had worked so hard to acquire was gone. I had nothing, and that was stressful. I was alone because my family was so far away. I was living in the basement of the local newspaper editor and manager of the weekend farmer's market. He let me live there for free because I was broke, out of options, and barely surviving.

The Phoenix Rises From the Ashes

In 2001, after I graduated from Ohio University, my live-in girlfriend left me shortly after an adventurous trip we took to visit national parks in the western part of the US and Canada. I was stuck in a small college town, still broke, lonely, and depressed. I worked as a food delivery driver for a submarine sandwich shop and a late-night calzone business. I delivered food to drunken frat and sorority houses till four in the morning every weekend and barely made enough money to pay for the gas in my car. Luckily, I knew a lot of kind, goodhearted folks who cared about me, but I didn't want to remain broke, unhappy, and aimless in my career.

At the tender age of twenty-one, I decided it was time to move back home to pursue a "real" career. I was ashamed, I was downtrodden, and I was out of work. I couldn't even afford Christmas gifts for my family that year. My parents, kind souls that they were, let me move back in with them while I tried to get a job in my career field, botany and medicinal plants, but it was an uphill climb, to say the least.

This was just after 9/11, and it appeared the chances of me finding a career path in my field that would pay me enough to survive were slim. It took me three months to realize this, however, before I finally took a position as a smoke-stack tester with an Environmental Air Pollution consulting company.

At the time, that job paid just enough—ten dollars an hour plus overtime. I was working day and night in all weather conditions—in drenching rain and icy snowstorms. I'd find myself swaying in blustery winds on top of hundred-foot smokestacks at manufacturing and incinerator plants throughout the Midwest. I worked fourteen-hour days, testing smoke stacks at companies like Avery Dennison, Mactac, LTV Steel, and the Cleveland Northeast Ohio Regional Sewer District Plant where they incinerated human waste—ewww! The job was stressful, intense, and unhealthy for my long-term health.

I was young and able, but after about a year of that work, I was beginning to realize it was *definitely* not my dream job. I had to make a change because I was feeling the effects of the stress, and the Crohn's disease was really starting to be a problem. Head hung low, dirty, and exhausted, I'd show up for dinner at my parents' dinner table about once a week. My parents didn't like seeing me like that. They hated that I was miserable, tired all the time, unhappy, and unhealthy from breathing in toxic chemicals all day.

After watching me show up at the dinner table for about year looking like I wasn't going to make it another day at my smokestack testing job, my dad turned to me one day and said, "Angelo, why don't you come work for me and run a desk?"

If you've ever had a chance to talk with my dad, Gary Giallombardo, on projects or on the phone, you know he's a great guy with a dynamic personality. I didn't have that type of personality, or so I thought.

I laughed and said, "I don't know, Dad. I don't have your personality, and I don't think I'd enjoy what you do."

After about three conversations with my dad, where in each one I insisted I wasn't cut out for the job, he sold me on an inside job working at a desk. At that point in my life, working inside was the only draw. A week later, I quit my job as a smokestack tester and joined Central Executive Search as a recruiter. This was one of the hardest decisions I've ever had to make. Jumping from a career where I *knew* how much money I was going to make into a career that paid me less but had more potential was a very scary proposition. It was a risk. A bold move. I wasn't sure of myself, but I went with my intuition. At the time, I just wasn't happy, and the risk outweighed the fear. Looking back, I realize that taking risks is a huge part of success. You have to be able to push all your chips into the center of the table, go all in, and let the cards fall as they may. Risk can be scary, but complacency can be stifling.

In high school, I had done a little bit of work for Central Executive Search. I filed papers in filing cabinets, scanned resumes, examined resumes and cover letters, and even answered a few phone calls. I still didn't know a damn thing about recruiting, and I knew it.

On my first day of work, I started off learning the recruiting side of the business from the boss and the other recruiters in the office. I thought I had it all figured out. I thought I knew everything there was to know about recruiting before I even tried it. I quickly learned that although I was comfortable in the office, I was green, and my confidence was low. I knew nothing about working with candidates and hiring managers, let alone how to run a desk. I didn't know the art of the deal or the pitfalls of running a desk in these markets.

In my early days at Central Executive Search, I was having success, but the Crohn's disease was getting worse. The culmination of making a career change, not taking care of myself in college, the unhealthy days at the smokestack testing job, and the stress of not making much money was compounding inside of me. I was losing weight rapidly, unable to eat and digest my food, and in constant pain. I knew I had to go through something big, but I was very scared to do so.

I decided it was time for surgery to repair the diseased part of my small intestine. I had been avoiding it for ten years, but I couldn't avoid it anymore. I didn't want to die, and I was starting to waste away. The surgery happened on my mom's birthday—May 20, 2004. They removed eighteen inches of scar tissue from my small intestine. It was an intense surgery, and it took me six months to recover. But recover, I did. I started to gain weight. I changed my diet and was able to exercise and grow again. It changed my body, my thoughts, my perspective, and my feeling about life. I became eternally grateful for the opportunity to be alive, the opportunity to grow into the person I wanted to be. My transformation had begun. A life of eternal gratitude is the mindset I still have to this very day.

At work, thankfully, I had one of the most successful mentors in the industry as my boss. I had the distinct advantage of learning, hands-on, from him. He was eager to teach, and I was stubborn yet willing. For the first few years, I was getting my feet wet, learning the ropes, and getting knocked around a lot, but I kept getting up and asking for more. Little did I know those early days of getting knocked down, punched around, failing, losing out on deals, facing rejection daily from the gatekeepers and hiring managers, and being called a number of four-letter words would be the foundation of a highly successful career and a long-term big biller.

> "I've come to believe that all my past failure and frustration were actually laying the foundation for all the understandings that have created the new level of living I now enjoy."
> – Tony Robbins

I share this short story of my growth as a person and in my career as a way for you to see that, just like you, I was once searching, digging, and scouring the world for my dream job. I had great potential but little understanding of what to do with it. I had solid training but little implementation and execution. I had some ambition but not enough foresight to see what I could become. I was lost in the woods until I found a home, a place that shared my values, guided me, nourished me, and brought me from a boy who didn't know what it was like to taste success to where I am now—a man who knows his potential is unlimited.

You too can find your home. You too can find your dream job. You too can unleash your potential and find that it's unlimited. With my help and experience, you can find your career home. With my experience working with candidates like you over the last fifteen years, you can find your ideal company match, your career calling, your place to flourish.

Through this program, my job is to guide you, to show you the ropes, to help you understand the mindset that will unleash your true potential and help you find the career of your dreams. It's all there for you. You just have to decide you're going to find it. You have to know it's already there for you, waiting for you take it. The first steps are simple—decide it's time, and determine *why* it's your time to make a move. *Why* you are making the decision must be as powerful and purposeful as my *why* when I was a broke twenty-one-year-old calzone delivery man.

You *will* have the career you dream of, but the first step is for you to DECIDE to take a risk. After making the decision to change, you must have ironclad faith and determination and never give up until your vision becomes reality.

Chapter 2

Your Strengths, Weaknesses, and Core Values

"My attitude is that if you push me towards something that you think is a weakness, then I will push that perceived weakness into a strength."
– Michael Jordan

We all have our strengths, and we all have our weaknesses. When I first started out, I didn't know my greatest strengths and weaknesses, nor my core values, and quite frankly, I didn't care. I soon discovered that I really needed to discover my strengths, my weaknesses, and my core values if I wanted to improve myself.

The process of landing the job you always wanted doesn't start with finding the opportunity you want to apply for. It starts when you decide to take that risk. Afterward, you need to look inside yourself and evaluate your strengths and weaknesses.

Self-actualization and self-realization are the greatest challenges we face in our lives, but the most rewarding. People who have mastered themselves are often the same people who have accomplished the most in their careers. In other words, when you don't know yourself, what you do best, and what you need to work on to get better, your chances of getting the job you want aren't very good.

Some candidates don't want to learn their core values, strengths, and weaknesses, some are afraid of them, and some just don't care. If you fall into one of these categories, I have a question for you. How do you expect a hiring manager to want to hire you if you aren't self-aware enough to know your own strengths and weaknesses?

"Your vision will become clear only when you can look into your own heart. Who looks outside, dreams; who looks inside, awakes."
– Carl Jung

One of the key elements to finding your next career opportunity is assessing your true strengths, weaknesses, and core values. I often advise people looking for a change to do several tasks that will help them identify their strengths. First and foremost, you should make a list of your strengths and weaknesses from your own point of view. Get out a piece of paper, divide it in half, and start listing your strengths first. I think you'll find that you have more strengths than you think. Follow that up with a list of your weaknesses. As you look over this information, understand that you might not know all of your own strengths and weaknesses.

The next step in identifying your strengths is to ask the people who are in your life on a daily basis about your strengths. Ask them to list your biggest strengths. Let them know this is for your own personal growth and development.

Often, they will be more than happy to help. If they don't want to help, you may want to evaluate whether they are truly people you want to keep in your life long term. The list of strengths your friends, family, and colleagues provide you is very important in understanding your positive attributes. These people often see your strengths more clearly than you do. Compare the lists and realize that if several people have listed the same strengths, these are likely your biggest strengths. After identifying the commonalities between their lists and your own, it's time to go to the next step in this process.

If you don't know your personality type or haven't taken a personality test, I encourage you to do some searching on the Internet. Take the time to evaluate yourself through free and paid online tools on the Internet. One of the best tools I've used over the last fifteen years is the Myers-Briggs test, but there are countless free tests online to assess your personality type and profile. The test results will show you your strengths, weaknesses, and core values, and they will, in turn, help you determine how to successfully present yourself to your interviewers.

Some of the free tests I've found online that I suggest you review are 16Personalities, Human Metrics, Truity, 123test, and the Who Am I? Quiz by Visual DNA.

Here is a list of the websites where you can access these tests:

https://www.123test.com/

https://www.16personalities.com/free-personality-test

http://www.humanmetrics.com/

You Got The Job!

http://www.truity.com/test/type-finder-research-edition

https://www.visualdna.com/quizzes/

Evaluating yourself and learning what you're best at and what you need to improve are important steps in being hired for your dream job. The hiring managers, interviewers, and colleagues you'll be working closely with are all interested in making sure they hire the right person for their company. To present yourself in the best way possible and make them believe you are the right person for the job, you'll have to show them you have the characteristics of the ideal employee for their team.

After you've had a chance to evaluate your strengths, weaknesses, and core values, you can learn how to maximize your potential in the interview setting. Maximizing your strengths and hiding your weaknesses in your resume will help you tremendously in the interview process. This takes a little bit of work on your end, but the results will be worth your time.

One of your main objectives is to highlight your strengths on your resume. Doing this will help get you in front of the decision-maker for the position. I'll talk more about resumes and how to put the ideal resume together for each position you apply for later in the book, but for now, the take-home message is to showcase your strengths in your resume.

"Success is achieved by developing our strengths, not by eliminating our weaknesses."
– Marilyn vos Savant

As far as your weaknesses go, it's obvious that you don't want to display them on your resume. It's important to know what your weaknesses are, however, because your interviewer will likely ask you about them at some point in the interview process. I'll address this later, but the key here is to be completely open and honest about your weaknesses and show the interviewer how you are working to turn them into future strengths.

The interviewer and hiring managers will most likely want to work with someone who is both honest and up-front about their challenges and weaknesses and working hard to turn those weaknesses into strengths. Self-realization and self-actualization are the keys to showcasing your ability to grow, change, and evolve into a better coworker, employee, and person. Employers will recognize your potential and see your ability to grow and become a true asset to their company and organization. When you take some time to figure out your core values, strengths, and weaknesses, you will be more likely to find the ideal company and work team match for the next successful venture in your career.

Chapter 3

Superhuman Confidence

Once you've had some time to learn about yourself, what makes you tick, what your core values are, and what your strengths and weaknesses are, the next step in your job search is to develop superhuman confidence. Often, when a job seeker is seeking their ideal career position, there's some self-doubt. This self-doubt takes different forms, and often we aren't even aware of it. One my mentors, Peter Voogd, once said, "One percent doubt, and you're out," and his words have stuck with me from that day on. What he was really talking about was the fact that if you don't have one hundred percent confidence in yourself, you can't expect someone else to see confidence as one of your major traits. The most successful people want to work with those who have a high level of success. Therefore, in your interview process, it's important to impart superhuman confidence, boundless faith, and an ironclad belief in yourself.

When I talk about superhuman confidence, some of you might snicker and laugh, thinking about comic book superheroes who don't exist in real life. Realistically, though, what superhuman confidence comes down to is focusing on a goal, envisioning yourself reaching that goal, and not letting any challenges, struggles, or people's opinions of you get in the way. There will always be people in your life who don't believe in you or your dreams. Some of the most successful people on the planet with billion dollar companies, organizations, and dreams have been told they couldn't do what they wanted to do.

Let's talk about my favorite sports superstar when I was a kid—Michael Jordan. When I was in grade school, I was a big Cleveland Cavaliers fan (because I was born in Cleveland), but I looked up to and followed Michael Jordan—even though he consistently beat my favorite team. Jordan seemed to have the ability to beat any single player or team at the end of a basketball game. He always made the shot no one else could seem to make. Often, it was the game-winning shot or the play that destroyed the dreams of the opposing team and their fans. For example, there was "the shot" on May 7, 1989, in the first round of the NBA playoffs. Michael Jordan crushed the dreams of the Cavaliers—and me, as a Cavalier fan—with a last-second, game-winning, buzzer-beating shot over a very good defensive player, Craig Ehlo. This wasn't the first time, nor the last time, that Michael Jordan would beat a team with his incredible skills and his confidence in his abilities.

Despite the fact that his shot brought to a halt the Cavaliers playoff run in 1989, I was still a huge Michael Jordan fan. I liked his superhuman confidence and his ability to make a shot at any time. The following year in fifth grade, I was doing a school project on people I looked up to. I began to study Michael Jordan. I read a book about his life and was shocked to find out that when he was in high school, his high school basketball coach cut him from the high school basketball team. He said Jordan wasn't "good enough" to play for the team. Despite his inability to make the team in high school, Jordan had an unstoppable work ethic, and he had confidence in himself. The rest is history as he went on to win six NBA titles and become arguably the best basketball player of all time. It was his skill combined with his strong self-confidence that helped shape his destiny. He was willing to take a risk, a shot, a play that others players weren't. That superhuman confidence made the difference in his career.

> "I've failed over and over in my life, and that is why I succeed."
> – Michael Jordan

The reason for this story is to showcase that we all fail, even the very best at their craft. The key is to learn from your failures, pick yourself up, and try once again. It's how we respond to failure that determines our successes. It's imperative that we develop the right mindset. The difference between how we view ourselves and how others view us is dependent upon how we respond to our failures.

If you are going to be the best version of yourself and find the best possible job in the next step in your career, you must develop the kind of superhuman confidence that says *nothing* will alter your path or deter you from accomplishing your goals. Focusing on your strengths and highlighting your positives are the keys to developing this kind of confidence. When adversity hits, your response to it will be crucial. To develop the confidence you will need to succeed, you must not allow (perceived) failures, negative situations, or negative feedback get to you and stop you from accomplishing your goals. Often, when the things we set out to accomplish don't happen in the way we want them to, we allow those situations to crush our self-confidence. Instead, when that happens, we must let go of the hurt and continue moving forward. Remember the old saying—when one door closes, another opens.

There is another major key to growing your personal confidence. It doesn't start one day when you wake up and decide to be confident going forward. Learning to be confident is a **process**, and I want to show you how you can implement this process. It boils down to *consistency* and *habits*.

Confidence begins within, that is clear. You have to show up every day in your life and be present and aware of your *own* thoughts. Self-awareness is crucial. If you want to develop a greater sense of self-awareness, I highly advise you to start a meditation or yoga practice and get some counseling to start working on the *inner* game in your mind and body.

Working out is very important in this endeavor. What we put into our mind and body has a direct correlation to our happiness. It's crucial to exercise and work out the toxins and built-up energy within. This will inspire you to reach for greater heights, enable you to see your true physical potential, and encourage your mind to be more positive. The saying "a healthy body equals a healthy mind" is correct. If you want your mind to think the best thoughts, working out daily or several times a week is very important.

You don't have to lift heavy weights or be a bodybuilder to get to a place of a more positive mental attitude. You do, however, have to give yourself a minimum of fifteen to twenty minutes of intense workout a day or several times a week. This will spark your mind to create more positive thoughts about yourself, which in turn will build your self-confidence.

Confidence is the consistent building up of self-esteem. You must practice building up your confidence through the habits in your life. The most positive habit is working out, but there are other habits that contribute to your confidence as well. I mentioned self-awareness and meditation. What you feed your mind daily will directly correlate to the amount and level of success you have in your job search. When you start thinking positive thoughts consistently, you will see better results.

Part of thinking positive thoughts is the practice of affirmations. Thinking positive thoughts every morning and evening, and actually speaking these positive thoughts out loud has a profound impact on your mental well-being. You begin to actually believe these thoughts and *act* on them. This creates a positive confidence loop that you will benefit from in your career advancement search process. Remember, you are an accumulation of your daily habits, so be aware of what you are thinking, feeling, and putting into your mind and body each day. This will give you excellent results over time.

Going back to your actual job search, there will be many resumes sent, many steps in the interview process to go through, and many interviewer's opinions and perceptions to overcome. It's your job to have—and display—superhuman confidence. Show the hiring managers that you will operate positively and productively in the role you are looking to take on. The way in which you respond to criticisms, problems, negative feedback, and lack of interest by a hiring manager will determine whether you reach your full potential and your goal of obtaining the position you've set out to get. No one wants an employee on their team who doesn't have faith in himself or who doesn't believe in the company's success. Being confident in the interview process shows the hiring manager you can handle the stress and challenges of the job.

There are countless resources and tools out there to aid you in developing that superhuman confidence. Many award-winning authors have published books to help you find confidence at work and accomplish your goals. Some of the better books and resources include *Confidence at Work: Get It, Feel It, Keep It* by Ros Taylor, *What's Holding You Back?* by Sam Horn, *Unstoppable Confidence* by Kent Sayre, and *The Ultimate Secrets of Total Self-Confidence: A Proven Formula That Has Worked for Thousands* by Dr. Robert Anthony. There are also many courses you can take and seminars and workshops you can attend. I encourage you to learn the secrets of building superhuman confidence if you wish to showcase this trait in your interview process. By training your mind to have this ultimate confidence, you will create the best possible version of yourself for your new employer.

"You gain strength, courage, and confidence by every experience in which you really stop to look fear in the face. You are able to say to yourself, 'I lived through this horror. I can take the next thing that comes along.'"
— Eleanor Roosevelt

Chapter 4

Correct Resume Writing

"The shorter and the plainer the better."
– Beatrix Potter

Part 1: Building the Resume Do's and Don'ts

A candidate calls me and asks me to review his resume and give him advice on it. I experience this scenario every day, and I'm happy to provide pointers and constructive criticism. Sometimes the resume looks good and needs only a few tweaks, but other times, the resume is a mess. Resume writing is an art, and many people don't understand its purpose. No matter what I say, some candidates just don't get it.

Resumes and cover letters are the main tools by which you can get the interview you want. So many people spend way too much time agonizing over their resume, forgetting that it's really a tool to obtain the interview. *Getting* the interview is the resume's main purpose. You don't get hired based on your resume. You get hired based on your personality, your credentials and accomplishments, your background, and your connection with the interview team. The resume and cover letter are there to open the door to the interview.

There are many tools and tactics you can use in building a resume and cover letter. In my experience, there are many do's and don'ts. Later in this chapter, I will list them for you, but for now, I'll describe the reasoning behind them so you can better understand *why* we are applying these methods.

When a hiring manager first peruses a resume, there are certain things he or she wants to learn about the candidate. The resume reflects the candidate's organizational skills, polish, professionalism, and experience in their career. It's important to understand you will be judged not only on the content, but also on the format.

> "The most valuable of all talents is that of never using two words when one will do."
> – Thomas Jefferson

The best advice for a building a resume is that it should be no more than one to two pages long. It should be short, concise, and direct. Hiring managers, HR professionals, and recruiters look through a lot of resumes each day, so it's best to keep it brief. It shouldn't be complicated. A good rule of thumb is that a high school student should be able to read and understand your experience after looking over the resume one time. Don't use a lot of fluff, adjectives, or filler to make your resume longer. That will only create more challenges for you to get the interview.

When you format a resume, it must look clean. You want it to have a simple yet organized structure. For example, you'll want your name, address, phone number, and email address centered on the page at the top of the resume. This is important because the hiring manager will have many resumes to look at, and your resume will need to stand out and be easily identifiable when this person is sifting through, reading, and organizing piles of resumes from prospective candidates.

After you have the top of your resume organized, you will want to be sure that the remainder is formatted in the same way. The margins and sections must be lined up correctly, and all of the information must be in the same format, font, and organizational style. For example, when you list your sections, make sure the font is the same size and color, and all in bold, underlined, or italics if you chose to use any of those options. It's almost always best to keep it simple with regards to font and style. Standing out and being different isn't always the best option on your resume—it's unnecessary, and the hiring managers know this.

There will likely be four major sections to your resume. The first section is the *Summary*. In the summary, your goal is to summarize your experience for the position you want to acquire. In this section, don't use first person words such as "I," "me," or "we." It's best to keep it general and describe yourself in the third person. For example, instead of saying, "I am an accomplished Sales Executive with proven experience in corrugated packaging markets," you should say, "A successful and accomplished Sales Executive with excellent, proven experience in corrugated packaging markets." This is a standard rule and has been part of resume-building as long as I've been in the business. I believe the reason for this is because when describing yourself and your experience, you don't want to seem conceited and sound like you're bragging about your accomplishments.

In summary, get to the point quickly. Keep it short and in the range of two to four sentences. Don't go into detail, and don't give numbers or statistics. Just describe your experience in your role with the company and list the markets in which you've worked and served and the products you've been involved with in your career.

Because each resume you write will be custom-tailored to the specific job you're looking to acquire, you will be able to adjust this section to describe your experience in the products and markets to suit the specific job for which you're applying. I will talk more about custom resumes later in the chapter.

The next section will be your *Experience*. This is where you will list your previous companies and your roles in those companies, your dates of employment, and a description of what you did in each position. Remember to keep the format, font, and spacing the same.

Under experience, you will list your company name, company location, and dates employed *all* on the first (first and second if it goes past the first) line. Below that line, you will talk about what the company does, makes, or sells and to what markets they sell. Keep it short and sweet, and no more than two to three sentences.

Underneath each company, list the different job roles you've had at that specific company. I would underline each job you've had and indent them to make it all uniform and set off from the line in which you listed the company. After the underlined job, and on the same line, provide the location of the job and the dates you worked in that job. Under that line, you will want to utilize bullet points or dashes to list your responsibilities, numbers and statistics, and the focus of your specific job role. If you had more than one role at a company, list them separately and describe your responsibilities, numbers, statistics, and focus under each one.

Many people make the mistake of listing a company more than once if they changed roles within that company or if the company was acquired. I would not advise doing this because, at first glance, it makes it look like you jumped to a new job when, in fact, you were at the same company but in a different role. Instead, on the company line, list the full amount of time you were at that company, and under the role, list the full time you were in that role in that company.

Once you finish your most recent company, you will follow suit with your previous companies and roles. Keep your list in chronological order, with the most recent company in your career at the top and the oldest company at the bottom.

The next section is *Awards and Accomplishments*. This section is simple. You use this section to list awards you've received and accomplishments you've experienced in your career. Again, don't speak of yourself in the first person. Use the third person so you don't appear to be boasting. If you wish, you can list your community involvement, volunteering, or any groups you are a part of in the awards and accomplishments section. You can list your industry associations in this section if it's relevant to the company and industry you're applying for. Don't list hobbies or what you like to do in your spare time.

The final section on your resume is your *Education*. This section's contents need no explanation. It's where you list your educational degree(s) or your experience in education. My advice is to list your advanced degree first (PhD or master's degree) and then your bachelor's degree under the advanced degree. If you have a college or associate's education degree, don't list your high school. If you do not have a college education, you should list only your high school and graduation date. If you have a vocational education degree, you can list that with your high school information.

One of the most important parts of your education section is the dates. It's a must to list the dates of your education. Often, if you're hired, the company will do a background check and call your school to find out if your degree is registered and valid. Do *not* lie about your degree. I've been in situations where a candidate was hired for a position, and the company called the college to ask about his or her degree, and it either wasn't valid or wasn't fully completed. The person didn't end up working for the company because they couldn't be trusted. If you lie on your resume, you are *not* going to get the job. Trust me, it's not worth it to stretch the truth about your education—it will come back to haunt you if you do.

"No one has a resume that they are 100% comfortable with, nor does anyone have a life that they are 100% comfortable with."
– Jay Baruchel

As a rule, do not lie about anything during the interview process. If a company wants to hire you, they will eventually find out, and when they do, and if you've lied, they won't be able to trust you. It's best to be authentic, up-front, and fully honest about everything or else run the risk of ruining your relationship with hiring managers, coworkers, and everyone in the company you wish to work with.

Some candidates want to list other parts of their lives on their resumes, such as their marriage, their kids, their hobbies, or the sports they're into. I would not advise adding things like this to your resume. It's simply not relevant to the person who is looking at your resume. This information will come out in the interview process, and it's best to wait until then because it's a great way to build rapport and communication, discuss commonalities, and build a relationship with the hiring manager. Saving this information for the interview process will help you gain the trust of the hiring manager and interviewer.

One of the major mistakes I see candidates make is sending a generic resume to *every* job they apply for. This is a problem because often the person is applying for a job unrelated to the past career roles they've had, or maybe they're applying for a job in an industry in which they have no experience. Generic resumes are recipes for disaster. For example, if I send resume for a position as a technical service rep to a hiring manager, and my resume is focused on the sales and marketing experience in my career, the hiring manager is going to toss the resume aside very quickly because it isn't relevant to their needs. The best practice in sending a resume is to make a *custom resume* for each job.

Designing a custom resume for each job for which you apply is the best way to secure an interview and get the interest of the hiring manager. It may take some additional time to put a custom resume together or tweak your current resume to focus on specific points for each position, company, and market, but it's the best way to show the hiring manager you're qualified for the opportunity. A custom resume is worth the time if you wish to secure an interview. If you really want to impress a hiring manager and get an interview, it's best to read over the job description details. After reading the details of the opportunity, you can use the same words, ideas, markets, and products in the job description in your resume to show the hiring manager you have the experience required for that specific opportunity.

The summary section is located at the top of the page and will catch the eye of the hiring manager right away. It is the first and most important section of your resume that you can customize and shape. If you use the exact words, ideas, and descriptions of job responsibilities as the opportunity you're applying for, the hiring manager will be more likely to continue reading and consider you for the role.

Again, and I can't state this enough, one pitfall to avoid is lying about your past experience and responsibilities. Even if you don't have the experience, responsibility, markets, or product knowledge the company is looking for, don't lie. Remember, you're looking to build your career with the best possible fit for your future, and lying on your resume is the first step in destroying that relationship you want to build.

"Lying can never save us from another lie."
– Vaclav Havel

Another reason to build a custom resume is to make sure the hiring manager, recruiter, or interviewer sees that you are putting forth a special effort for this specific opportunity. It shows you've done your research, put in some time, and care enough about the opportunity to spend the extra time to create a special resume for that specific position. It also paints a vivid picture of how you will work in your role with the company.

As far as generic resumes, they're good for online profiles on job boards, forums, or other public sites. They're also good for public speaking events or public forums to describe what you've accomplished in your career. The audience will want to know more about your career focus and experience. The generic resume is also a good starting point from which to make a custom resume for each specific opportunity you hope to acquire.

One of the most important parts of the resume writing process is *quantifying* your experience and results. There is nothing worse than reading over a resume where there are no numbers, statistics, or percentages to help the hiring manager understand the success the employee has had in previous positions. It's best to include numbers and statistics for each position in which you've worked because it will be a major selling point to get the interview. We all want people on our team with proven successes, and quantifying your success is the easiest way for hiring managers to see just how much success you've had in your career. It's a *must* to do this on your resume.

Lastly, while writing your resume, you will want to think about the references you will provide on a separate document. You need to contact three to five business-related references. The reason you must contact them is to let them know about your job search and ask them if they are willing to answer some questions from the hiring managers at the company to which you are applying. Let the references know you will be happy to do the same for them when the time comes for them to search for a new position. Once they have agreed, list their names, titles, the companies they work for, and their full contact information. This will be helpful to the hiring manager or human resource executive when they begin contacting references later in the hiring process.

"In my early professional years, I was asking the question: How can I treat, or cure, or change this person? Now I would phrase the question in this way: How can I provide a relationship which this person may use for his own personal growth?"
– Carl Rogers

Resume Writing Do's and Don'ts

Do:

➢ Keep it short and direct.

➢ Make it clean, and be sure it is uniformly formatted.

➢ List the company you worked for *only* once.

➢ Include Summary, Experience, Awards & Accomplishments, and Education sections.

➢ Include dates for your specific company *and* roles within that company.

➢ Include date of graduation in your Education section.

➢ Quantify results in your Summary, Experience, and Awards & Accomplishments section!

➢ Create custom resumes for each specific job you apply for.

Don't:

➢ Use too many adjectives or descriptive words.

➢ Use run-on sentences.

➢ Have more than one to two pages in your resume.

➢ Lie or exaggerate your experience, accomplishments, or education in any part of your resume.

➢ List jobs or roles in your experience *without* dates.

➢ List your education *without* dates.

➢ Send a generic resume for each specific role you are applying for.

Part 2: Cover Letters: Do's and Don'ts

We haven't yet touched on cover letters, and they're an important part of putting together a custom resume for each career opportunity you apply for. There are a lot of reasons to write a good cover letter for the opportunity you're seeking. Cover letters show the hiring manager you are going to put maximum time and effort into the tasks you wish to accomplish. They also help the hiring manager see your organization for the task at hand.

There are a few do's and don'ts that go along with writing the cover letter. Get to the point! Cover letters often drag on. The first sentence is very important. It shows the hiring manager or recruiter that you are going to be direct in your approach. Don't start your letter with a drawn-out, compound idea and an overworked sentence. You should express only one idea and thought in the first sentence. Another thing to keep in mind is that the cover letter shouldn't be too much fluff. Keep your adjectives to a minimum, and keep your thoughts focused. It's important to quantify your results, but don't go overboard with a ton of statistics. One major mistake in the cover letter is that it goes on and on. Keep it to a paragraph or two with approximately three to four sentences per paragraph. It should end quickly, or it won't be something the hiring managers will want to read. Remember, their time is important, and they live by the same rule you do—time is money. Lastly, at the end of the cover letter, make sure you make it a point to indirectly ask for what you are seeking—a job interview. Tell them you want to move on to the next step, and show them how you can help the company. Offer your experience, accomplishments, and qualifications—direct and to the point —and your cover letter will be a success.

"Emphasize your strengths on your resume, in your cover letters, and in your interviews. It may sound obvious, but you'd be surprised how many people simply list everything they've ever done. Convey your passion and link your strengths to measurable results. Employers and interviewers love concrete data."
– Marcus Buckingham

Do:

➤ Include one idea or thought in the opening sentence of the cover letter.

➤ Include a custom cover letter for each job you apply for.

➤ Keep it short and get directly to the point.

➤ Keep it to two to four sentences in each paragraph, only two to four paragraphs.

➤ *Quantify* your results.

➤ Ask for the interview or make it clear you believe you are qualified for the position.

➤ Contact your references and list their titles, companies, and contact information.

Don't:

- ➤ Send a generic cover letter for each job you apply for.
- ➤ Use run-on sentences or too many adjectives.
- ➤ Make the cover letter more than one page.
- ➤ Talk about results and accomplishments without numerical data to back it up.
- ➤ Write a cover letter without asking for the interview.
- ➤ Imply you aren't sure if you are qualified enough.

Part 3: Sample Resumes and Cover Letters

CONSULTATIVE SALES
GREENSBURG, PA 12345

consult12@comcast.net   123.456.7890   linkedin.com/in/consultativesales

---

CONSULTATIVE SALES / BRAND POSITIONING & DEVELOPMENT / MERCHANDISING – POG DESIGN
DISTRIBUTOR MANAGEMENT / TRAINING & DEVELOPMENT / STRATEGY & RELATIONSHIPS

Proven Consumer Goods Sales Executive with exceptional talent for building and nurturing relationships with key decision makers. Astute, strategic consultant who delivers ethical and trusted business advice, representing the industry's leading brands to drive growth and profitability. Certified Retail Selling Skills Instructor who utilizes training, experience and creative leadership to develop and hone team talent while consistently delivering exceptional customer service through a polished, professional image.

KEY STRENGTHS:

Strategist | Complex Negotiator | Brand Positioning | Creative Leadership | Distributor Management
Training & Development | B2B & B2C Communications | Budgeting | Consultative Sales | Multi-Location Management
Relationship Management | Merchandising/POG Design | Key Account Management | Public Speaking/Presentations

CAREER ACCOMPLISHMENTS

- **STRATEGIC DEVELOPMENT & EXPANSION** – Realized 6% sales increase in 2014 through nurturing 250 single- and multi-store regional accounts within $6MM sales territory. Facilitated all management/distributorship oversight and direction with on-going growth and successes.

- **DYNAMIC LEADERSHIP & OVERSIGHT** – Instrumental in maintaining key retailers' marketplace leadership positions through direct management of 2 regional multi-store chains, utilizing expertise in account development tools such as trade-spend investments, associate training, new product presentations, POG design, planned business reviews and credit processing. Utilized leadership and training expertise to maximize operational efficiencies and consistently provide a positive and unique customer experience.

> "Chris took over an undeveloped New England of the three upper states and made it a pivotal area for the whole Eastern United States. Chris is an extraordinarily gifted sales manager. Understated, but able to bond quickly and deliver real value to his retailers as well as being a fantastic employee to supervise."

- **ASTUTE BUSINESS MANAGEMENT EXECUTIVE** – Successfully presented product seminars to retail store associates and conducted Retail Selling Skills seminar modules to develop internal talent on various key business management strategies, increasing product recommendations and delivering sound advice to retail partners while adhering to corporate ROI expectations.

PROFESSIONAL HISTORY

Mars PetCare, Greensburg, PA
Territory Manager
1995 - 2014

Promoted and managed territory that included Maine and New Hampshire through face-to-face B2B communications and product promotion to regional chains, independent stores and local Petcos and PetsMarts. Grew territory for premium pet food products from infancy to 300-product portfolio with 20% market share through educating account managers and differentiating products from competitors through quality demonstrations and value-added customer service.

- Visionary leader who served on Field Marketing Advisory Board, guiding market strategy for deeper market penetration and driving new product roll-outs.
- Delivered value-added customer service by training store staff on the features, benefits and merchandising strategies of Mars products, including delivering seminars on aspects of achieving better sales and delivering better customer service techniques.

RICHARD J. CELENTANO

Mars PetCare (Cont'd.)
- Provided strategic business planning and operational oversight by focusing on long-term business relationships. Utilized business acumen to advise contacts on industry insight and improving store revenue streams. Provided contract representatives for weekend public outreach initiatives to increase store traffic and increase Mars product sales. Provided direct solutions to store owners/managers, compelling them to carry and promote Mars products.
- Achieved 50% margins on Greenies products (pet dental products), impacting customer product mixes by recommending product and maintaining strong site presence in each location.
- Established Mars as a market leader by educating on product lines, designing displays, performing compliance checks and delivering hands-on product demonstrations.
- Effectively communicated with key internal and external sources, consistently collaborating on all lines to foster relationship building and educate on product lines.

Kraft Foods, Inc., Pittsburgh, PA
Sales Representative
1994 - 1995
Creative and strategic representative, instrumental in roll-out of Tombstone Pizza to local chains and establishments.
- Deployed all phases of promotions to grow new product line from infancy to $1MM in annual sales.
- Executive command of product, development and promotions to deliver brand growth.
- Effective verbal and written communicator, consistently updated key stakeholders on strategies and merchandising plans.
- Fostered & developed relationships to generate/maintain key relations with distributors, new business and key accounts.

Color Performance Painting Company, Color, NH
Owner
Successfully executed entrepreneurial, management and administrative tasks, including establishing budgets and cost controls, ensuring price accuracy, margin analyses, inventory management and human resources functions, for new enterprise, growing operations to $200,000 in annual revenue.
- Ensured smooth daily operations, including securing new business, delivering contracted services, developing community presence and professional public image, and identifying and developing key talent.
- Consistently utilized business acumen to provide accurate forecasting and budgeting, forecasting and inventory management.

EDUCATION

Bachelor of Science (B.S.), Business Administration – Plymouth State University, Plymouth, NH

HONORS & ACHIEVEMENTS

Employee Engagement Champion Team Leader, 2012 – 2014
Field Sales Onboarding Mentor, 2012 – 2014
Field Marketing Advisor Board, 2010 – 2012
Associate Engagement Champion for Northeast Sales Team, 2012
Organizer, Mars Volunteer Program Events, 2008 - 2012
Featured on Nutro Focus on dotMars, "A Day in the Life of a Nutro Sales Territory Manager," 2011
Most Creative, Pet Food Peddler Seminar Award, 2009
Independent Retail Sales Nomination, National Make the Difference Award, 2009
Best Territory Northeast Award, 2007
Territory Sales Growth Master, New England Independent Retail Division, 2004 – 2006
Best Overall Territory, New England Independent Retail Division, 2002
Salesperson of the Region, New England Independent Retail Division, 2001
District Manager of the Year, United States Winner, 2001
Sales Achievement Award, New Product Retail Placement, 1997

Obviously, your background will be somewhat different from the fictitious one presented here. Include such things as products, processes, machine familiarity, special techniques, etc. that may interest a prospective employer.

Correct Resume Writing

Sample Technical Resume:

Vishal Arupo

12345 Ventura Blvd., Apt. 204 ■ Encino, CA 91436 ■ Cell: 123.1234.0000 ■ Vishal.Arupo@netvega.com

SOFTWARE ENGINEERING EXECUTIVE

EMERGING TECHNOLOGY ■ PRODUCT ENGINEERING ■ ENTERPRISE SOFTWARE DEVELOPMENT ■ QA MANAGEMENT

Transforming software engineering through the integration of next generation technologies and tools.

- Software Engineering Executive who leverages exceptional business acumen, technical expertise, and 40+ team management success, to conceptualize/execute strategies and software programs that support/drive company growth.

- Consistently offer practical IT quality solutions that positively impact profitability, control costs, and optimize resource utilization; translate business needs into actionable product solutions.

- Extensive experience enhancing systems and on- and off-shore personnel performance with advanced platforms, budget management, and cutting-edge solutions that address strategic business organization requirements.

- Skilled IT executive who inspires internal and external teams to achieve corporate goals and follow through with assignments utilizing sound problem resolution expertise. Proficient in SaaS, Web design/development, and QA Management initiatives.

- Actively seeking greater leadership challenges within an organization poised for growth, where excellence in Agile, SCRUM, iterative software development and continuous integration/delivery techniques are held at a premium.

■ LEADERSHIP AREAS OF STRENGTH ■

- 14 Years QA/Software/Web Design & Development
- Exceptional Project Management Leadership/Direction
- Quality Assurance/Software Testing/QA Management
- Test Infrastructure/Automation Engineering
- Recruit/Train Top Tier Engineering Teams
- Strategic Planning and Management

- Large 40+ Team Management
- Operations/Capital Budget Management
- Design/Develop QA/Test Methodologies
- Devise Quality Assurance Processes/Procedures
- Analytical Planning / Sound Troubleshooting Skills
- Onshore/Offshore Product Engineering

 QUALIFICATIONS PROFILE

- Develop, lead and manage high performance engineering and QA teams within multiple sites in product engineering within numerous industries that include financial services, telecom, transportation, utilities, Internet, new product development and e-Business.

- Drive IT direction and delivery on software development projects and serve as hands-on project management for test development and production testing including testing optimization, vendor management and delivery on cost effective scheduling and budget constraints for each project.

- Leverage operations and business acumen, methods and metrics, serving as an innovative problem resolutions expert utilizing advanced analytical, planning, scheduling focused on time/budget delivery excellence skills.

- Spearhead quality assurance processes/methodologies, project/test planning and infrastructure, as well as test plan development, test case/data review and effective test automation practices.

EXECUTIVE EXPERIENCE

2013 to Present: Condusiv Technologies, Burbank, CA – Director of Quality Assurance
Direct and provide leadership for a QA division in a high profile technology organization that design and develops high-performance software optimizing technology that supports system optimization and performance that extends equipment longevity for increased business performance and continuity, with annual revenue of $400MM.

- Evaluated new technology and seamlessly implemented technology and tools that provided QA organizational development/delivery.
- Began tenure with 5 direct reports and drove software expansion success necessitates hiring of 10+ additional QA engineers involved in high profile commercial and OEM applications and systems software development that meets/exceeds client business requirements.
- Identify and evaluate new/emerging technologies, procure and implement new technology tools that provide QA organization best practices.

Page 1 of 3

You Got The Job!

- Perform critical review of business requirements deficiencies, gaps in technical specifications, designs and testing documentation that ensures accurate and complete testing environments.
- Manage QA team scheduling, track and report on software testing progress and identify and share QA and testing metrics with business units and IT C-level executives.
- Champion development and delivery of SQA and testing policies/procedures, as well as (SOP) Standard Operating Procedures.

2012 to 2013: Mitchell International – Senior Manager – SQA Engineering

Managed all facets of QA engineering and analysis for a leading provider of Workers' Compensation cost containment, technology and solutions in response to client and market driven requirements. Utilized continuous integration and delivery standards and led a team of 20+ QA engineers and analysts; drove execution planning and delivery of software QA best practices.

- Identified, analyzed and assessed QA strategy, architecture, gaps. Improved planning and development; championed QA automation efforts that improved testing cycle times.
- Monitored and assessed QA efforts, identified deficiencies in cycle and elapsed times and designed effective plan of action that improved manual testing efforts.
- Completed QA testing early in development phase and ensured review by development and BA teams; implemented metrics improvements ensuring greater compliance with corporate guidelines and business standards.
- Improved department processes/procedures focused on operational efficiency communicated QA team alignment with company goals and drove continuous talent management of QA team—served as technical/functional leader that assisted in performance growth and adaptation to changing processes.
- Managed onshore/offshore contractor quality assurance teams.
- Utilized Lean/Agile methodologies in the organization's transition into the current business process.

2011 to 2012: ARINC, Inc. - Senior Manager, Quality Assurance

Drove quality assurance excellence for an organization that developed advanced railroad communications and control systems that included positive train controls (PTC); for a $100MM contract that provided services to 3 major railroads—recruited to turnaround product failure, completed on time for this highly sophisticated software railroad solution.

- Monitored and developed software QA operations, software controls and delivery; performed key client consultation and strategic negotiations in preparation of software specifications, proposal presentation and engineering reports/findings.
- Managed 16 engineers within the QA Department and assigned/reviewed all technical production standards and assisted in deficiencies as needed.
- Developed QA Dashboard for executive leadership team.

2010 to 2011: Symantec Corporation – Manager, SQA Engineering

Developed and directed high performance onshore/offshore software development teams for the Online Licensing Platform group and planned, directed, and evaluated activities and operations focused on quality control and system performance assurance success for renowned Symantec.

- Designed and delivered QA standards, policies/procedures for engineering and technical work within the department and assigned, coordinated and reviewed all work performance of department and assigned project teams.
- Recruited, trained and developed new personnel; led team in the design and development of QA tools and technologies.
- Built state-of-the-art automation infrastructure that significantly improved QA capability for continuous delivery by achieving operational efficiency.

2008 to 2010: Avanade Inc. – Global Quality Assurance Manager / QA Architect

Managed global team collaboration and delivery for multiproduct teams of 40+ team members in production of enterprise business solutions in meeting global division quality mandate. Developed comprehensive testing methods, test tools and technologies utilizing Microsoft stack and created and delivered QA processes/procedures, metrics and standard practices.

- Fostered a strong team collaboration process in design/implementation of V-model testing methodologies for enterprise clients, estimated, scheduled, resources planning and managed testing efforts for future engagements and monitored/tracked test progress for internal/external releases.
- Maintained cost effective scheduling and project quality initiatives that ensured on time and budget client project delivery—drove effective customer satisfaction levels through sound software QA process development.

Correct Resume Writing

Vishal Arupa

2003 to 2008: Microsoft Corporation – SDET II / SDET Lead
Office Communication Server / Technology, Care and Safety (TCS) / MSN Entertainment
Directed design and development of test plan/cases, functional integration/regression and complete testing through software automation rollout; developed design processes, testing infrastructure and tools for team members and oversaw design spec review, test design processes and creation of automation procedures.
- Documented security guidelines for core server team, investigated/defined security requirements and tools for each team and drove critical security testing for each featured area.

Completed projects included:
- Office communication server - Rich Presence and Conferencing.
- Designed/developed test tools and technologies (e.g. SIPTest – SIP Client Tool allowed communicating with server. Widely used by development/testing for debugging issues).
- Team Engineering Excellence focused on productivity, efficiency and quality.
- SIP Protocol Compliance Verification and Technical Documentation.

EARLY CAREER (1998 TO 2003)
Sr. Programmer / Project Lead – Innosoft, Inc.
Project: Innosoft Web Portal design/development.
Sr. Web Programmer – ZONES, Inc.
Consultant – International Software Consulting, Inc.
Programmer - Masum Technologies Pvt. Ltd.

EDUCATION / CERTIFICATIONS

M.S., Computer Science – New York Institute of Technology, New York, NY
B.Sc., Computer Technology – YCCE, Indiana – Honours Graduate

Certification
2011: 81st Technology Management Program – University of California Los Angeles, CA
2008: Managing for High Performance – University of Washington, Seattle, WA
2005: Design Firm leadership and Management – University of Washington, Seattle, WA
2005: Effective Communications & Human Relations – Dale Carnegie Course

Publications, Patents and Awards
Article: Unique Value Proposition through Customized Solutions & Services!! - Silicon India Magazine – July 2013 issue
SAFECall – Mobile Child Safety Solution, Defensive publication on IP.com { IPCOM000152466D} on 5/4/2007
SAFECall – Mobile Child Safety Solution, Patented on 5/4/2007
Microsoft Gold Star Award Recipient – 2008

Technical Proficiencies

Programming Languages:	C# | .NET | C/C++ | Java | PHP | PL/SQL | Pascal | Assembly 8085/8086
Web Tech/Platforms:	SaaS | SOA | ASP.NET | ADO.NET | ASP 3.0 | HTML 4.0/5.0 | XML/XSLT | SOAP UDDI | WSDL | Java/Shell Script | Apache | IIS | BroadVision 6.0 | Power Shell
Software Solutions:	Visual Studio.Net | VB.NET | .NET Framework | Dynamics CRM/AX | SharePoint 2010 Power Builder 5.0 | Dreamweaver | MS DRM | Windows Installer | MS Project | Clarion
Database Solutions:	SQL Server 2008 R2/2012 | Oracle 9i/10g | MySQL | SQL Anywhere | Big Data MS Access | E-R Win | Toad
Operating Systems:	Microsoft Windows | Linux | IOS | Android | Solaris | UNIX
QA Tools and Technologies:	Microsoft TFS | Test Manager | Selenium | QTP 11 | QC 10 | Load Runner 10 | eTrack Product Studio | FxCop | Cenzic Hailstorm | NCover | YSlow | PageSpeed | nUnit DynaTrace | Jira | SOAP UI | Fiddler | Toro
Configuration Management:	Microsoft TFS | Visual Source Safe | Borland StarTeam | Perforce

Obviously, your background will be somewhat different from the fictitious one presented here. Including different industry and technical knowledge. It was also include such things as products, processes, machine familiarity, special techniques, etc. that may interest a prospective employer.

You Got The Job!

Sample Cover Letter & Resumes by Harvard Extension School:

Extension School

Resumes and Cover Letters

Harvard

OFFICE OF CAREER SERVICES
Harvard University · Faculty of Arts and Sciences
www.ocs.fas.harvard.edu

CAREER AND ACADEMIC RESOURCE CENTER
Harvard Extension School
www.extension.harvard.edu/resources/career-academic-resource-center

RESUMES
and
COVER LETTERS

An Extension School Resource

Correct Resume Writing

Office of Career Services
Harvard University
Faculty of Arts & Sciences
Cambridge, MA 02138
Phone: (617) 495-2595
www.ocs.fas.harvard.edu

You Got The Job!

CREATE A STRONG RESUME

A resume is a brief, informative summary of your abilities, education, and experience. It should highlight your strongest assets and skills, and differentiate you from other candidates seeking similar positions. Although it alone will not get you a job or internship, a good resume is an important element toward obtaining an interview.

Tailor your resume to the type of position you are seeking. This does not mean that all of your work history must relate directly, but your resume should reflect the kind of skills the employer would value.

NEED HELP?

- **CARC Resume and Cover Letter Webinar.** Learn the nuts and bolts of getting started. See the CARC or OCS websites for dates.
- **HES Call-ins.** First Monday of the month, Sep-May, 1:00-3:45pm (15 minutes). **Phone** (617-496-8946) or **Skype** (linda.spencer. at.ocs) during call-in hours only. Available to currently registered Extension School students and alumni only.
- **Career Advising Appointment.** Matriculated degree students and alumni only.

RESUME TIPS

RESUME LANGUAGE SHOULD BE:
- Specific rather than general
- Active rather than passive
- Written to express not impress
- Articulate rather than "flowery"
- Fact-based (quantify and qualify)
- Written for people who scan quickly

DON'T:
- Use personal pronouns (such as I)
- Abbreviate
- Use a narrative style
- Number or letter categories
- Use slang or colloquialisms
- Include a picture
- Include age or sex
- List references
- Start each line with a date

TOP 5 RESUME MISTAKES:
1. Spelling and grammar errors
2. Missing email and phone information
3. Using passive language instead of "action" words
4. Not well organized, concise, or easy to skim
5. Too long

DO:
- Be consistent in format and content
- Make it easy to read and follow, balancing white space
- Use consistent spacing, underlining, italics, bold, and capitalization for emphasis
- List headings (such as Experience) in order of importance
- Within headings, list information in reverse chronological order (most recent first)
- Avoid information gaps such as a missing summer
- Be sure that your formatting translated properly if converted to a .pdf

PLAN TO WORK INTERNATIONALLY?
Resume guidelines can vary from country to country. Check out GoinGlobal at http://www.ocs.fas.harvard.edu/going-global

Correct Resume Writing

ACTION VERBS FOR YOUR RESUME

LEADERSHIP

Accomplished	Achieved	Administered	Analyzed	Assigned	Attained	Chaired	Consolidated
Contracted	Coordinated	Delegated	Developed	Directed	Earned	Evaluated	Executed
Handled	Headed	Impacted	Improved	Increased	Led	Mastered	Orchestrated
Organized	Oversaw	Planned	Predicted	Prioritized	Produced	Proved	Recommended
Regulated	Reorganized	Reviewed	Scheduled	Spearheaded	Strengthened	Supervised	Surpassed

COMMUNICATION

Addressed	Arbitrated	Arranged	Authored	Collaborated	Convinced	Corresponded	Delivered
Developed	Directed	Documented	Drafted	Edited	Energized	Enlisted	Formulated
Influenced	Interpreted	Lectured	Liaised	Mediated	Moderated	Negotiated	Persuaded
Presented	Promoted	Publicized	Reconciled	Recruited	Reported	Rewrote	Spoke
Suggested	Synthesized	Translated	Verbalized	Wrote			

RESEARCH

Clarified	Collected	Concluded	Conducted	Constructed	Critiqued	Derived	Determined
Diagnosed	Discovered	Evaluated	Examined	Extracted	Formed	Identified	Inspected
Interpreted	Interviewed	Investigated	Modeled	Organized	Resolved	Reviewed	Summarized
Surveyed	Systematized	Tested					

TECHNICAL

Assembled	Built	Calculated	Computed	Designed	Devised	Engineered	Fabricated
Installed	Maintained	Operated	Optimized	Overhauled	Programmed	Remodeled	Repaired
Solved	Standardized	Streamlined	Upgraded				

TEACHING

Adapted	Advised	Clarified	Coached	Communicated	Coordinated	Demystified	Developed
Enabled	Encouraged	Evaluated	Explained	Facilitated	Guided	Informed	Instructed
Persuaded	Set Goals	Stimulated	Studied	Taught	Trained		

QUANTITATIVE

Administered	Allocated	Analyzed	Appraised	Audited	Balanced	Budgeted	Calculated
Computed	Developed	Forecasted	Managed	Marketed	Maximized	Minimized	Planned
Projected	Researched						

CREATIVE

Acted	Composed	Conceived	Conceptualized	Created	Customized	Designed	Developed
Directed	Established	Fashioned	Founded	Illustrated	Initiated	Instituted	Integrated
Introduced	Invented	Originated	Performed	Planned	Published	Redesigned	Revised
Revitalized	Shaped	Visualized					

HELPING

Assessed	Assisted	Clarified	Coached	Counseled	Demonstrated	Diagnosed	Educated
Enhanced	Expedited	Facilitated	Familiarized	Guided	Motivated	Participated	Proposed
Provided	Referred	Rehabilitated	Represented	Served	Supported		

ORGANIZATIONAL

Approved	Accelerated	Added	Arranged	Broadened	Cataloged	Centralized	Changed
Classified	Collected	Compiled	Completed	Controlled	Defined	Dispatched	Executed
Expanded	Gained	Gathered	Generated	Implemented	Inspected	Launched	Monitored
Operated	Organized	Prepared	Processed	Purchased	Recorded	Reduced	Reinforced
Retrieved	Screened	Selected	Simplified	Sold	Specified	Stored	Structured
Systematized	Tabulated	Unified	Updated	Utilized	Validated	Verified	

47

You Got The Job!

Sample Resume

Jin Wang
wang@gmail.com • (213) 555-6666

Education

Harvard University, Extension School
Master of Liberal Arts, Information Management Systems   May 2016
GPA 4.0
- Class Marshall Award
- Dean's List Academic Achievement Award
- Data Science Project: Financial Market Analysis Using Machine Learning
- Capstone Project: Enterprise Data Lake

University of Malaya
Bachelor of Computer Science   June 2008

Technical Skills

• Machine Learning	• Python/Scikit-learn	• Spark	• Data Visualization
• Quantitative Analysis	• Cloud Computing	• Hadoop	• Java/C#
• Unix Scripting	• Oracle/SQL Server	• PLSQL/T-SQL	• Data Warehouse/ETL
• RDBMS Tuning	• Network Protocals	• Agile & DevOps	• Web Development

Professional Experience

Rande Corporate & Investment Banking   Detroit, MI
Associate – Information Technology   September 2013 – Present
- Lead a team of 6 people to manage, operate, and support low latency post-trade brokerage platform
- Improved the performance of straight-through processing by tuning database applications
- Reduced number of major incidents by 23% through problem management
- Automated manual back-office processing through scripting and automation engine
- Actively participated and contributed to the internal data science project initiatives

Olson Financial   Singapore
Associate – Information Technology   February 2011-September 2013
- Built a new application support team of 5 people focusing on post-trading straight-through processing and data warehouse extract-transform-load processing
- Designed and implemented global application monitoring platform.
- Eliminated 80% of manual checks for trading support, and decreased SLA breaches for client reporting by 15%

SAMPLE RESUME (page 2)

PS Engineering Information Ltd.   Singapore
Software Developer – Technology Office   July 2010 – January 2011
- Built Command & Control System for Singapore Civil Defence Force using C# .NET WCF Services
- Integrated proprietary software components with commercial off-the-shell software product

Well   Beijing, China
Software Developer   June 2009 – June 2010
- Built supply chain management system using Java Spring/Hibernate Framework and Service Oriented Architecture
- Improved the performance of real-time business activity monitoring report and reduce the report response time by more than 50%

Silver Technologies Ltd.   Singapore
Software Developer   May 2008 – May 2009
- Developed web-based Point of Sale (POS) application using C# .NET for a multinational fashion retailor
- Researched and implemented RFID authentication software module

Certifications

- 4-course graduate-level certificate in Data Science, Harvard University   January 2016
- ITIL Foundation V3   January 2015
- Project Management Professional (PMP)*   March 2013
- Certified Salesforce Developer   October 2012

49

You Got The Job!

SAMPLE RESUME

Nadia Smythe
smythe@g.harvard.edu | 444-555-2222
linkedin.com/in/nadiasmythe/

EDUCATION

HARVARD UNIVERSITY EXTENSION SCHOOL   2014 - 2016
Master of Liberal Arts, Management
- Recipient of Dean's List Academic Achievement Award
- Selected for the Venture Incubation Program at Harvard Innovation Lab and winner of Stretch Award 2016

UNIVERSIDAD NACIONAL AUTONOMA DE MEXICO   2001- 2006
Bachelor of Business Administration in Marketing
- Graduated from Honors Program, Rank 1
- College Student of the year 2006 awarded by Expansion Time Warner Magazine
- Recipient of L'Oréal Excellence Award 2006

PROFESSIONAL EXPERIENCE

AGENDA28   September 2012- Present
CO-FOUNDER/ DESIGN STRATEGY DIRECTOR
- Founded design studio specialized in social impact that develops integral design strategies to increase effectiveness of social initiatives and empowers young designers from underserved communities in Mexico
- Led 20 design projects for nonprofits and social enterprises in the U.S., Mexico, India, Zambia, Australia, Switzerland
- Won Most Innovative Idea at Educational Innovation and Social Entrepreneurship Conference at Harvard - May 2015

ENTERPRISSE DE MEXICO   November 2008 - January 2014
MARKETING & SALES DIRECTOR
- Led the Marketing and Sales teams achieving a company growth of 163% in 5 years
- Reinforced the brand by redesigning the corporate identity and executing online marketing campaigns
- Improved the customer service by implementing a new Sales Methodology, a CRM and a Loyalty Program
- Developed a new Corporate Strategic Planning methodology and coordinated all related activities
- Expanded operations to 9 new countries in Latin America

OPTICIANE MEXICO   January 2008 - October 2008
PR & MEDIA EXECUTIVE
- Managed the PR activities for 16 eyewear brands
- Planned events for Tiffany, Chanel, and Ralph Lauren winning best congress planner 2008 (Convenciones Mag.)
- Coordinated media campaigns for RayBan, Vogue and Prada
- Accomplished $1,300,000 USD in Clipping (free advertisement)

CLAIROLE MEXICO   March 2006 – December 2007
PREFERENCE BRAND MANAGER
- Performed the marketing activities including forecasts, new products launch, advertisement and promotions
- Led the Casting Crème Gloss and Color Rays market research
- Achieved 15% in annual growth vs 0.5% budgeted
TRAINEE: Managed the Mexico City's point of sales team
INTERNSHIP: Supported Paris' hair color brands with sales forecasts, design of promotions and PR events

VOLUNTEER EXPERIENCE

- **INCUBATEC**- Mexico City (January 2005 - May 2006): Coordinator of entrepreneurs program
- **ARTE NAJEL**- Chiapas, Mexico (July 2005 – March 2006): Marketing advisor for fair trade project
- **POLE**- Nairobi, Kenya (August 2012): Assistance to Mercy Community School to develop business plan

Correct Resume Writing

SAMPLE RESUME

Jesse Jayant
511-555-7777 / Jesse.Jayant@post.harvard.edu

Summary

Results-oriented finance professional with over 9 years of experience in publicly traded and privately held enterprises. Proven track record in complex and capital-intensive global industries, delivering value and innovation in Finance, Strategy, and Corporate Planning.

Core Competencies

- Financial Analysis
- Forecasting
- M&A
- Budgeting
- Business Planning
- Financial Modeling
- Strategic Planning
- Reporting
- Valuation
- Month-End Close
- Capital Planning
- Project Planning

Experience

USA Airlines, Chicago, IL
Sr. Financial Analyst, Information Technology Financial Planning   2011 - 2015
- Developed and monitored a $1B annual Information Technology (IT) budget.
- Tracked spending against budget and project progress to ensure effectiveness of financial controls and accuracy.
- Prepared and presented monthly, quarterly, and annual spending reports to CIO.
- Implemented new technology (SharePoint Portal) and processes to facilitate monthly reporting that decreased reporting cycle by over 40%.
- Constructed a comprehensive monthly forecasting model to reduce forecast cycle time from 2 weeks to under 4 days.
- As a member of USA's Chapter 11 Restructuring Team, conducted sensitivity analysis to re-negotiate 30 IT vendor contracts that resulted in 15% savings.

Dream Properties, Bangalore, India
Sr. Financial Analyst, Finance & Strategic Planning   2010 - 2011
- Analyzed and recommended to the CFO and CEO viable business investments in Real Estate projects and lease commitments ($5M-$25M).
- Identified redundancy in processes and personnel that allowed $3M of annual expenses to become a source of revenue.
- Led a team of 7 professionals to identify revenue potential and optimization as key drivers of future portfolio strategy.

USA Airlines, Chicago, IL
Sr. Financial Analyst, Human Resources Finance   2009 - 2010
- Divisional controller, leading financial reporting and analysis, accounting, budgeting, P&L optimization for $200M HR division including Compensation, Vendor Management, Retirement.
- Led effort to right-size USA's unionized workforce. Reduced total headcount by approximately 800 FTEs, resulting in annualized savings of $60M.
- Modeled and presented the financial structure of USA's variable compensation & bonus plans to executive management.

Sr. Financial Analyst, Operations Business Planning   2008 - 2009
- Directed the implementation of a $50M technology project at over 10 major US Airports (including Dallas/Fort Worth, Chicago, New York, Miami, Los Angeles) that scaled to support over 15,000 employees, increased productivity by 12%, and reduced lost baggage expenses by 8%.
- Built the Checked Baggage Fees Model and projected revenue stream ($12M) by forecasting the change in passengers' baggage check-in behavior.
- Developed an optimization model to define refurbishment strategy for over 300 ground service equipment that led to $2M savings.
- Designed USA's Rent Pricing Model to determine lease commitments for all US airports.

USA Owl Airlines, Chicago, IL
Financial Analyst, Financial Analysis & Capital Planning   2006 - 2007
- As a member of the Finance Integration Team, collaborated with Merrill Lynch to develop a spinoff report to provide guidance and enable departments estimate post spin-off revenue and cost synergies.
- Assessed departmental needs and partnered with internal customers on the composition of USA's capital plan for 2008 ($500M).
- Served as a liaison between Corporate Planning and Capital Planning, analyzed and acquired funding of $120M for large capital projects in 1 year.
- Identified and implemented cost-saving initiatives of $250K through ground service equipment optimization at 60 US airports.

You Got The Job!

SAMPLE RESUME (page 2)

Alpro Laboratories, Detroit, MI   2006 - 2006
Financial Analyst, Finance & Business Planning
- Re-designed the revenue forecast model to reduce budget preparation time by 30% in 4 months.
- Analyzed and recommended the CFO to adjust product production based on competing companies' market share for multiple product lines.

Morgan Firm, Wood, MI   2005 - 2005
Intern
- Assisted portfolio managers in analyzing stocks and mutual funds for prospective and existing clients
- Participated in client financial planning discussions and quarterly portfolio review.

Education
Harvard University, Extension School, Cambridge, MA   May 2016
Master of Liberal Arts - Management
- Dean's List, GPA 3.89

Kalamazoo College, Kalamazoo, MI   December 2005
Bachelor of Business Administration - Finance
- Summa Cum Laude, Dean's List, GPA 3.92

Additional Information
- **Cultural Experiences:** Visited over 30 countries in 4 continents and lived in 3 countries
- **Social Impact:** Susan G. Komen Walk Fundraising – Member (2012-2013), Mother Teresa Missionaries of Charity – Committee Member (2010-2011), Big Brother Big Sister – Member (2008)
- **Personal Interests:** Avid reader, traveller, bicyclist

Correct Resume Writing

SAMPLE RESUME

Jacob A. McLean

1921 Rainy Day Drive • Cambridge, MA 02140
jacob.mclean@post.harvard.edu • (617) 555-3456

Education

HARVARD UNIVERSITY Extension School   May 2015
Master of Liberal Arts, Information Management Systems

- Dean's List Academic Achievement Award recipient
- Relevant coursework: Trends in Enterprise Information Systems, Principles of Finance, Data mining and Forecast Management, Resource Planning and Allocation Management, Simulation for Managerial Decision Making

RUTGERS, THE STATE UNIVERSITY OF NEW JERSEY   May 2008
Bachelor of Arts in Computer Science with Mathematics minor

Professional Experience

STATE STREET CORPORATION   Boston, MA
Principal - Simulated Technology   December 2011 – July 2013
- Led 8 cross functional, geographically dispersed teams to support quality for the reporting system
- Improved process efficiency 75% by standardizing end to end project management workflow
- Reduced application testing time 30% by automating shorter testing phases for off cycle projects
- Conducted industry research on third-party testing tools and prepared recommendations for maximum return on investment

FIDELITY INVESTMENTS   Boston, MA
Associate – Interactive Technology   January 2009 – November 2011
- Initiated automated testing efforts that reduced post production defects by 40%
- Implemented initiatives to reduce overall project time frames by involving quality team members early in the Software Development Life Cycle iterations
- Developed a systematic approach to organize and document the requirements of the to-be-system
- Provided leadership to off-shore tech teams via training and analyzing business requirements

L.L. BEAN, INC.   Freeport, ME
IT Consultant   June 2008 – December 2009
- Collaborated closely with the business teams to streamline production release strategy plans
- Managed team of five test engineers to develop data driven framework that increased application testing depth and breadth by 150%
- Generated statistical analysis of quality and requirements traceability matrices to determine the linear relationship of development time frames to defect identification and subsequent resolution
- Led walkthroughs with project stakeholders to set expectations and milestones for the project team

Technical Expertise

MS Excel, PowerPoint, Relational Databases, Project Management, Quantitative Analysis, SQL, Java

Additional

Organized computer and English literacy workshops for underprivileged children in South Asia, 2013
Student Scholarship Recipient, National Conference on Race and Ethnicity, 2007-2008

You Got The Job!

SAMPLE RESUME

SUSAN R. SMITH
2 Kinnaird St. • Cambridge, MA 02139 • 781.555.7777 • ssmith@post.harvard.edu

EDUCATION

Master of Liberal Arts, Finance
Harvard University, Extension School, Cambridge, MA (May 2016, GPA 3.85)

Bachelor of Science, Biomedical Engineering

Carnegie Mellon University, Pittsburgh, PA (December 2003, GPA 3.76)

Level II Candidate CFA Program

PORTFOLIO MANAGEMENT PROJECT

HARVARD UNIVERSITY - Investment Management Course   Spring 2014
Final project (Bill and Melinda Gates Foundation Asset Trust)
- Group leader and Fixed Income manager
- Diversified portfolio achieved a risk - adjusted 11% annual return, preserving wealth and satisfying yearly distribution goals
- Usage of Black-Litterman and Mean-Variance Optimization modeling and Bloomberg database
- Team ranked highest among all groups of the Investment Management class

PROFESSIONAL EXPERIENCE

SYNOPSIS, INC., MARLBOROUGH, MA   2011 – Present
Senior Application Consultant II - Synplicite Product Sales

Synopsis is a publicly-traded provider of software for ASIC and FPGA microchip design serving Fortune 500 companies. Synopsis purchased Synplicite in 2008.

Demonstrated Revenue Growth:
- Earned 120% of quota via pivotal technology solutions and key relationships
- Achieved 150% of quota in 10 month period by expanding product usage

Proven Leadership:
- Implemented synthesis flow for top storage provider, resulting in client's record purchase of Synpliclite products
- Selected by senior management to support eastern Canada accounts and assist team in growing FPGA business
- Selected as Synplicite Track Leader for Boston Synopsis User Group event with 400+ clients, team earned top rank
- Lifted team capabilities, personally identifying and hiring new application consultant

Technology Investment Management:
- Year-over-year proven results and support reliability resulted in tier one customers increasing their annual, multi-million dollar software investment by 24%

SYNPLICITE, INC., ANDOVER, MA   2003 – 2011
Senior Field Application Engineer - Synplicite Product Sales

Demonstrated Revenue Growth:
- Consistently triggered revenue growth, generating 20% sales growth for 5 consecutive years
- Increased military account booking by 50%, by establishing product value and performance

Technology Investment Management:
- Recommendations, results, and proven support record resulted in industry leading storage and router firms to transition to new microchips and software across their entire product lines

Proven Leadership:
- Recognized by executive management for building excellent relationships with top accounts and industry partners and for positioning solutions versus leading competitors
- Drove development and implementation of top selling features for structured ASIC and verification software
- Eliminated competition at critical accounts and averted ASIC designer division layoff for telecommunication provider
- Collaborated with teammates and marketing management to uncover new business opportunities and strengthen relationships with high-profile military, telecommunication, processor, and storage accounts
- Promoted to Senior Field Application Engineer
- Promoted to Field Application Engineer
- Hired after completing challenging summer internship, quickly developed expertise in digital design languages

Correct Resume Writing

<small>SAMPLE RESUME</small>

SANJAY GOPAL

75 Smith Lane • Billerica, MA 01821 • 978-555-9999 • Sanjaygopal@gmail.com

---

Project Director

A results oriented Project Director with extensive leadership experience in highly competitive IT and Telecom industry. Proven track record of leading and managing multi-million dollar international programs across northern Europe, Middle-East, North America and South America.

Specialize in launching new services and products from concept to roll-out and building organizations from ground up. Expertise in improving team performance while securing customer loyalty and forging valuable relationships with internal and external partners.

Core Competencies

Project/Operations Management	Leadership	P&L Management
Strategic Planning	Building organizations	Risk Management
Client Management & Retention	Negotiations	Business development

Professional Experience

Comverse Inc., USA   Oct 2007 - Present
The world's leading provider of Telecom software and systems

Project Director / Consulting Program Manager, Boston / London / Dubai
Delivered 30+ Projects and Programs within agreed budget, time and quality for telecom operators in North America, South America, northern Europe and Middle East region. Planned & supervised "concept to launch" for enterprise software systems, system integration projects for telecom operators in voice, data & billing domains. Prepared service proposals, RFP responses & worked closely with sales groups to secure new business.

Accomplishments:
- Delivered 30+ projects valued 80+ Million USD, on-time, within budget with team of up to 100 people for Verizon Wireless, Sprint, Bell Canada (North American clients), America-Movil, Millicom (South American clients), Vodafone, Orange, (European Clients), Q-Tel and Etisalat (Middle Eastern clients).
- Introduced Visual Voice Mail services for Verizon wireless nationwide in aggressive schedule with team of 100+ professionals.
- Managed launch of first Ring Back tone project for Sprint within very demanding timeframe. Comverse was awarded multiple expansions based on success of project.
- Coordinated very competitive trials for multiple services for Bell Canada and won the contract.
- Launched a globally distributed ring back tone service for Orange Global in UK, France and Belgium. Team consisted of 100+ team members including Sub-contractor (Cap-Gemini).
- Introduced new product lines across North America, Europe and Latin America.
- Built and managed Comverse (Middle East) organization from scratch to team of 4 Project managers and 13 Engineers.

55

You Got The Job!

SAMPLE RESUME (page 2)

Atlas Telecommunications, UAE   April 2006 - Sept 2007
Leading telecomm solution & system supplier, based in UAE

Business Development Manager, Abu-Dhabi
Marketed and sold telecommunication systems for Telecom, Defense, Oil and gas companies. Managed contract negotiations, RFI /RFP responses and project agreements.

Accomplishments:
- Exceeded the sales target for 2002 and 2003 by 25% (3.6 Million USD).
- Successfully introduced and won projects for Mera systems, Scientific South and Comverse Inc.

Facile Call Paging, India   June 2004 - March 2006
Largest & most innovative paging service provider in India

Sr. Manager (Projects & Operations), New Delhi
Launched first green field paging network across north India. Managed operations and customer support with team of 9 engineers and 70 customer care agents.

Accomplishments:
- Built Facile Call technical organization from ground up across 7 locations in India.
- Member of core team to bid nationwide spectrum auctions and vendor selection.
- Launched and managed green field paging services across major cities in demanding time scales.

Education

Harvard University Extension School, Master of Liberal Arts, Management, Expected May 2017

Regional Engineering College, Surat, India, Bachelor of Engineering, May 2004 **Project**

Management Institute (PMI), Professional Certification: PMP

Sanjay Gopal   [2]

56

Correct Resume Writing

SAMPLE RESUME

John Reynolds
17 Reed St. • Boston, MA 02118
jreynolds@post.harvard.edu • 617.555.6543

Education

HARVARD UNIVERSITY Extension School, Master of Liberal Arts, Biotechnology (May 2015)

- Relevant coursework: Business Analysis and Valuation, Entrepreneurial Leadership, Biostatistics, Clinical Trials and Regulatory Issues, Project Management
- Thesis: Assessing Acquisition Potential in the Medical Technology Market
- Faculty Aide Program: received a $500 stipend for research investigating medical technology

UNIVERSITY OF FLORIDA, Bachelor of Science in Neurobiological Sciences (May 2008)
- Florida Bright Futures Award recipient: Full academic scholarship (2003-2008)
- Interdisciplinary Studies scholar with a concentration in Behavioral Neuroscience (Senior Thesis on abnormal repetitive behaviors in mice)
- Graduated from Honors Program

Professional Experience

BRIGHAM AND WOMEN'S HOSPITAL - Boston, MA (December 2009 - May 2015)
Senior Research Assistant
- Create and maintain computer databases for statistical analyses
- Prepare presentations, manuscripts, abstracts, and book chapters for publication
- Perform technical duties for clinical studies in the field of sleep medicine and cardiovascular health
- Redesigned and updated the Medical Chronobiology Program Web site

HARVARD UNIVERSITY - Cambridge, MA (January 2011 – May 2011; January 2012 – May 2012)
Teaching Fellow for the course, BIOS E-210, "The Physiology of Sleep"
- Prepared syllabus and created course materials
- Designed course Web site, led discussion sections, maintained correspondence with graduate students
- Organized guest lectures featuring several prominent researchers in the field of sleep medicine

WGBH EDUCATIONAL FOUNDATION - Boston, MA (August 2011 – January 2012)
Project Consultant for the HMS Sleep and Health Education Web site
- Conducted literature reviews and produced original multimedia content based on current research
- Reviewed site content to determine scientific accuracy

HARVARD MEDICAL SCHOOL - Boston, MA (March 2011 – January 2012)
Assistant Editor for the HMS Sleep and Health Education Web site
- Developed and revised scope and architecture of the site

Publications

Sleep Research Society: Lee, S. & Smith, W. (Co-developers: Lee, S. & **Reynolds, J.**) (2014). Fundamentals of the circadian system. In C. Amlaner, & O. Buxton, (Eds.), *SRS Basics of Sleep Guide*

Abstract: Neil, L., Jones, R., Lopez, A., **Reynolds, J.** (2014) Lack of Endogenous Circadian Rhythm of Platelet Aggregability. *SLEEP 2014 (Conference)*

Community Service

Big Brothers Big Sisters of Massachusetts Bay: Serve in both the school-based and community-based mentoring program in Dorchester, MA

You Got The Job!

SAMPLE RESUME

Elizabeth Wong
212-555-1333
ewong@post.harvard.edu

EDUCATION

Harvard University Extension School, Cambridge, MA — November 2016
Master of Liberal Arts, Foreign Literature, Language, & Culture, GPA: 3.8
Recipient of Dean's Outstanding Achievement Award

Harvard University - Summer Abroad Program, Prague, Czech Republic — Summer 2012

DePaul University, Chicago, IL — May 2006
Bachelor of Arts, Journalism, Minor in Communications & Culture

EXPERIENCE

Harvard Kennedy School of Government, Cambridge, MA — January 2014 – April 2016
Admissions Assistant
- Worked closely with Assistant Directors and Deans of Admissions, handled highly confidential materials and assisted with processing over 2,000 applications

CL English, London, UK — Summer 2013
Teacher
- Taught English as a foreign language to 32 international university students

Harvard Business School, Boston, MA — May 2009 – June 2013
Faculty Assistant
- Managed first year required course MBA curricula for four professors; oversaw all updates to online syllabus; organized business case edits; assisted students; ordered publications and materials for research/courses; processed new publications, individual research, communications, and supplemental class materials; managed all travel and expense arrangements
- Coordinated annual unit conference for 60+ MBA professors nationwide; designed and oversaw conference website; communicated with potential attendees; collaborated with HBS faculty and potential presenters
- Interacted with a diverse group of professors, executives and students

Westfield Concession Management, Inc., Boston, MA — April 2007 – May 2009
Marketing Manager
- Supported 30 airport retailers with all real estate concerns, daily operations, and related issues concerning maximization of sales. General annual retail sales average $14 million
- Created Incentive Program for managers to motivate and credit staff. Served as interim general manager for six month period
- Organized airport marketing, promotional, advertising events and newsletter. Created and collaborated with advertising agencies to produce sales campaigns seen by thousands of potential customers
- Traveled nationwide to provide marketing and administrative assistance for new airport projects

Labouré College, Dorchester, MA — September 2008 – December 2008
Adjunct Instructor
- Taught core writing course to college freshmen

American Red Cross Campaigns, Boston, MA — October 2006 – January 2007
Assistant to Director
- Represented agency and organized large fundraising events throughout major venues in Boston and vicinity

SKILLS

Word, Excel, PowerPoint, Oracle, Outlook, Eudora, Photo Editor, PeopleSoft, Banner, Embark, Exeter, Conversational Spanish

Sample Resume

Sarah Lopes Jones

23 South St. • Concord, MA 01742 • 978-333-9898 • sljones@post.harvard.edu

Summary

- Accomplished Certified Project Management Professional with extensive experience managing project teams in all phases of the Software Development Life Cycle, as well as in infrastructure implementations.
- Proven track record of initiating and delivering successful projects to improve systems and performance in large complex development and production environments.

Experience

IBM, Cambridge, MA, 2004 - 2014
Senior Technical Services Professional, 2006 - 2014
IBM Software Group (SWG) HQ division, which manages services to 7 brands/divisions, including: Lotus, Rational, Tivoli, Cognos, and WebSphere, with a total client base of 35,000.

- Simultaneously led 3 cross-matrix teams of 5-15 members each, in projects to research, develop, and deliver yearly software development capital forecast plans. Total budget for all 7 divisions $100M.
- Saved an estimated $2M yearly by increasing productivity of 600 employees. Organized the development and implementation of a worldwide database application, including requirements gathering, development, UA testing, rollout, and training. Directed 4 major version upgrades. Considered "best in breed" application by IBM managers.
- Developed and managed a $30M yearly IT spending budget split between 35 groups/divisions located in 10 different European countries.
- Saved $8M/yearly by initiating and managing a project to transition all US datacenters to standardized servers. Prepared and maintained 25 cutting-edge configurations available by a single part number and delivered fully assembled.
- Managed relationships with Sun Microsystems and Hewlett Packard, to provide ongoing discounts on a variety of servers needed for SWG development.
- Insured compliance for Sarbanes Oxley audits by establishing and maintaining an out-of-cycle capital approval process. Authorized over $50M in requests yearly.
- Created the first standardized high-end ThinkPad to meet the needs of the Software Group developer community. Within 6 months this standard was adopted by all of IBM.
- Saved an estimate of $2M/yearly by reducing capital expenditure through cross-lab sharing and reuse. Member of *The Asset Reutilization Council*, and founder of *The Asset Sharing Database*.

Advanced Systems Management Integration Professional, 2004 - 2006

- Managed deployment projects specializing in security and systems management software throughout the Cambridge data center (200+ servers).
- Specified, ordered, loaded, and installed Windows data center servers as lead MS Certified Systems Engineer on internal project teams.
- Published white papers, processes, procedures, and work instructions for IBM on OS and software standards.

SAMPLE RESUME (page 2)

Sarah Lopes Jones   *page 2*

MJ Research (currently Bio-Rad Laboratories), Waltham, MA
Network Administrator and Help Desk Manager, 2001 - 2004

- Managed infrastructure projects, including: setup of multi-site DSL; DHCP and NAT conversion; SMS rollout; firewall installation; email migration; web server launch; database design; license server implementation; sales database rollout; VPN integration across WAN; Intranet design and installation in DMZ.

- Supervised helpdesk and staff. Prioritized help desk issues. Handled problem escalation.

- Directed selection, installation, administration, maintenance, upgrades, and backups for critical Windows servers on a cross-platform LAN/WAN with 200 nodes, and 50 remote users.

- Specified, ordered, installed, and distributed Macintosh systems to new hires. Trained employees on usage, company computer policy, and procedure.

- Held internal training classes in computer use, software applications, Internet, and project management.

Technical Skills

Hardware: IBM System x, BladeCenter, Intellistation, ThinkPad, PowerBook, AMD, Dell, Cisco, TotalStorage, NAS, tape backup.
Networking: switches/hubs, cabling, DSL/VPN, TCP/IP, remote access, DMZ/firewall.
Software: Windows Operating Systems, Mac OS X, VMware, security and virus protection, system mgmt software, middleware, BrioQuery, ACT!, Filemaker Pro, Eudora Pro, *Apple:* iLife, iWork. *Microsoft:* Office, FrontPage, Project, SMS, Outlook, Visio. *Lotus:* Notes, Symphony, Sametime, SmartSuite, *Adobe:* Photoshop, Illustrator, PageMaker, Acrobat.

Education

Harvard University Extension School, Cambridge, MA
   Master of Liberal Arts, Management, May 2015
Emerson College, Boston MA
   Bachelor of Science in Marketing Communications: Advertising and Public Relations, May 2001
PMI Institute: PMP Certified
IBM: Leadership Excellence Program: 148 class hours developing leadership skills
Microsoft: Windows 2000 Certified Systems Engineer

Correct Resume Writing

SAMPLE RESUME

Georgina Santiago
35 Lee St. Apt. 3 Cambridge, MA 02139/617-555-2212/gsantiago@post.harvard.edu

EDUCATION

Harvard University Extension School   Cambridge, MA
Bachelor of Liberal Arts, Field of Study Economics   May 2016
Cum Laude, Dean's List, GPA 3.62
Worked up to 40+ hours a week to defray cost of tuition

EXPERIENCE

Hangtime Wholesale Wine Company   Boston, MA
Sales Representative   2013-present
Opened and maintain 40 accounts in the greater Boston area. Conduct in-store tastings and staff
trainings to generate greater revenue. Create and distribute promotional materials.

Christie's Auction House   New York, NY
Intern, Fine and Rare Wine Department   2013
Performed pre-and post-sale statistical analysis. Researched and executed mass mailing in order
to generate new consignments. Researched potential domestic clients for annual Hospice de
Beaune Auction. Generated contracts for consignors. Served as front-line contact for both
existing clients and potential consignors, handling incoming and outgoing correspondence.
Compiled and entered tasting notes for auction catalogue.

Montagna Bar and Restaurant   Aspen, CO
Back-Server, Cocktail Server, Food-Runner   2013
Active participant in wine program, including weekly blind-tastings. Created suitable beverage
pairing for patrons.

Shay's Pub and Wine Bar   Cambridge, MA
Server, Bartender, Floor Manager   2006-2013
Coordinated and promoted weekly specials to generate optimal revenue. Participated in
development, expansion and improvement of wine program. Recruited and trained all floor
staff. Increased overall restaurant sales by 75%.

The Second Glass   Boston, MA
Staff Writer   2011-2013
Launched premier issue of print and online wine magazine. Increased public visibility through
participation in wine related events. Provided up to three articles per print issue and once weekly
for online issue. Conducted research and interviews for articles.

Certifications: Court of Master Sommeliers: Introductory Course
                     WSET Level 3 Advanced Certificate in Wine and Spirits (Pass with Merit)
                     Paris Chamber of Commerce and Industry Diploma in Business French
                     Member, Boston Sommelier Society

Volunteer: Domaine Carrett Bully, France 2013: Vineyard and Cellar Management
                     Ovid Vineyards, St Helena, California 2013: Office and Events Support

You Got The Job!

WRITE AN EFFECTIVE COVER LETTER

Your cover letter is a writing sample and a part of the screening process. By putting your best foot forward, you can increase your chances of being interviewed. A good way to create a response-producing cover letter is to highlight your skills or experiences that are most applicable to the job or industry and to tailor the letter to the specific organization you are applying to.

Your Street Address
City, State, Zip Code

Date of Letter

Use complete title and address. — Contact Name
Contact Title
Company Name
Street Address
City, State, Zip Code

Address to a particular person if possible and remember to use a colon. — **Dear ....:**

Opening paragraph: Clearly state why you are writing, name the position or type of work you're exploring and, where applicable, how you heard about the person or organization.

Make the addressee want to read your resume. Be brief, but specific. — **Middle paragraph(s):** Explain why you are interested in this employer and your reasons for desiring this type of work. If you've had relevant school or work experience, be sure to point it out with one or two key examples; but do not reiterate your entire resume. Emphasize skills or abilities that relate to the job. Be sure to do this in a confident manner and remember that the reader will view your letter as an example of your writing skills.

Ask for a meeting and remember to follow up — **Closing paragraph:** Reiterate your interest in the position, and your enthusiasm for using your skills to contribute to the work of the organization. Thank the reader for his/her consideration of your application, and end by stating that you look forward to further discuss the position.

Always sign letters. — Sincerely,

Your name typed

Some general rules about letters:

- Address your letters to a specific person if you can.
- Tailor your letters to specific situations or organizations by doing research before writing your letters.
- Keep letters concise and factual, **no more than a single page.** Avoid flowery language.
- Give examples that support your skills and qualifications.
- Put yourself in the reader's shoes. What can you write that will convince the reader that you are ready and able to do the job?
- Don't overuse the pronoun "I".

- Remember that this is a marketing tool. Use lots of action words.
- Have an OCS adviser proofread your letter.
- If converting to a .pdf, check that your formatting translated correctly.
- Reference skills or experiences from the job description and draw connections to your credentials.
- Make sure your resume and cover letter are prepared with the same font type and size.

Correct Resume Writing

SAMPLE COVER LETTER

February 21, 2016

Ms. Liza Wideman
Recruiting Coordinator
Great Strategy Consulting Firm
200 Shell Fish Blvd, Suite 199
San Francisco, CA 94080

Dear Ms. Wideman:

I am writing to express my interest in securing an Associate position at Great Strategy Consulting Firm. I am a Master of Liberal Arts degree candidate at Harvard Extension School, specializing in Information Technology. I come from a solid technical background with a strong interest in business and a passion towards strategy. My area of focus and interest varies from quantitative analysis to project management. I have maintained a 3.95 GPA through a well-balanced program of study, which is not only very analytical and technical by nature but also helps to build leadership and team building qualities. I am extremely impressed with Great Strategy's approach to strategy consulting, especially within the Business Development and Innovation practice areas. I believe my academic background, business knowledge and industry experiences have provided me with the credentials needed to thrive as an Associate.

Prior to Harvard, I worked as a technology professional, primarily resolving strategic issues related to technology process improvement. I gained solid research, analytical and problem solving skills while working in Fortune 500 companies. My background in generating innovative ideas and strategies to improve processes has provided me with a deeper understanding of multifaceted problems that companies encounter in their daily operations. Moreover, because of my work experiences, I fully understand how important it is to have great team dynamics in today's multi-disciplinary business environment.

To date, my experience as an IT professional has been extremely rewarding and productive. However, it is through strategy consulting that I can use my analytical aptitude and creative problem solving skills to their fullest. I strongly believe that consulting is a discipline that will force me to view problems not only from the client's standpoint but also from a marketplace, best practices and "think out of the box" point of views.

I would appreciate the opportunity to interview with Great Strategy Consulting Firm for the Associate position. Please find enclosed my resume for your review. I can be reached via email at jacob.mclean@post.harvard.edu or by phone at (617) 555-3456. I enthusiastically look forward to hearing from you soon.

Thank you for your time and consideration.

Sincerely,

Jacob A. McLean

You Got The Job!

SAMPLE COVER LETTER

October 10, 2016

Ms. Susan Carey
Senior Manager
Wholesale Wine USA
23 Green St.
Boston, MA 02116

Dear Ms. Carey:

I am writing to apply for your position in wine wholesale as advertised on Crimson Careers. This exciting opportunity appears to be a wonderful fit with my professional experience, personal interests, and career goals.

I am returning to Boston to complete my final year at Harvard University Extension School, where I am majoring in French and economics. Having spent the year working and traveling, I am eager to incorporate myself once again into the local wine community, to which I can bring experience in a number of sectors of the industry.

Through eight years in the restaurant field, I have acquired a deep love of and appreciation for wine and cuisine. I have been known to wax rhapsodic over specials; nothing made me happier than discussing a bottle with a table. This enthusiasm allowed me to introduce a list of reserve selections to Shay's Pub and Wine Bar. The result was an appreciable increase in sales for the restaurant and repeat attendance by customers. My position at Aspen's award-winning Montagna allowed me to expand upon my knowledge of wine, locally inspired cuisine, and the highest standards of service. Our weekly blind-tastings fueled my desire to further myself in this field, and I am in the process of acquiring certification through both the Court of Master Sommeliers and the Wine Spirit and Education Trust.

Most recently, I have returned from France where I was lucky enough to work on an organic vineyard in Beaujolais. I adored working with the young, dynamic, vigneron who ran the estate, the largest of its kind in the region. A position at your wholesale wine company would allow me to draw upon this experience and to facilitate the success of such producers. Additionally, it would enable me to replicate the most enjoyable components of my experience overall: working with my colleagues in the local restaurant industry, as well as with distinctive, iconoclastic wine-makers.

I am readily available via email or phone in order to arrange an interview, and have attached my resume below per your request. Please do not hesitate to contact me if you have any questions. I appreciate your consideration and look forward to hearing from you.

Sincerely,

Georgina Santiago

This is just a great resource with excellent examples of cover letters and resumes by a leading authority.

Chapter 5

The Job Search & Application Process

"The only way to find great work is to love what you do. If you haven't found it yet, keep looking. Don't settle."

– Steve Jobs

If you think applying for the job you always wanted will be a piece of cake, you'd better think again. Unfortunately, the job search, the application process, and engaging with the hiring team—everyone from the gatekeeper to the hiring manager—isn't as easy as pie. There are a lot of steps to consider when starting to look for your dream job. Taking in all the steps and processes can be overwhelming, but I will break down the most important steps in the process so you can maximize your time and efforts in finding the right opportunity for yourself.

Figuring out what jobs you are qualified for and can apply for is a basic first step. As a rule of thumb, if you have not worked in a particular role, haven't had exposure to it, or haven't had hands-on experience in the area you wish to pursue, you might not want to consider that opportunity at this stage in your career. For example, if you want to become a purchasing manager, but you only have experience in R&D chemistry on the lab bench without ever having been exposed in any capacity to purchasing, procurement, the supply chain, or material purchasing at your company, you may be wasting your time pursuing that role. You definitely want to stick with opportunities in areas you've either had exposure to or direct experience with in your company. Employers won't see the value in hiring you for a job in which you have no past experience.

The next step is figuring out how best to search for the position you're looking for. There are seemingly thousands of job titles, opportunities, and companies out there looking to hire. Filtering through the ones that both apply to your background and are interesting to you will be daunting. As a general rule, you must simplify the search process.

This time in history is the best and easiest time ever to search for a job. The opportunities available online are quite bountiful if you know how to search. There are quite a few different online companies, tools, and resources at your disposal. Some of the best tools I've found for searching for a job are LinkedIn, Monster, Career Builder, Indeed, and Zip Recruiter.

I'll start with LinkedIn because I believe it to be the most valuable resource available online. What started off as a professional networking site idea in 2002 has quickly become the best resource to find a job opportunity—*if* you currently have a job or have already established connections within the professional world. The concept of LinkedIn is simple—create a profile, follow up with detailed information on your profile, network with professionals you have had interactions with in the past, and begin to talk to professionals who can aim you in the right direction in your job search.

LinkedIn is a great place showcase your talents, skills, and detailed experience for the world to see. Make sure you fill out as many details as you can. Also, to get the most out of it, you will want to connect with as many people as possible. Join groups and exchange ideas and information. There are also some very good job opportunities on LinkedIn to explore. A lot of companies' human resources departments are using LinkedIn now, so take advantage of this bountiful resource by remaining active and applying for jobs that you are interested in exploring.

The Indeed job search site is a place to search for many jobs all at once. When you put your location, job title, and keywords into the search engineer, Indeed pulls up a bunch of different jobs that match your input. You'll find that a lot of recruiters often post their jobs. Be cautious and wary of some of these postings because there are times that the postings are outdated or just a lure to get you to send your resume to the recruiter for his or her database for the future. Many times, there are direct companies looking for candidates and advertising on the site. Be selective and only apply for jobs posted by direct hiring companies. By doing so, your chances of getting an interview will increase. Use the provided filters to narrow down your job search. This will help you pinpoint only the top few jobs that will be the best fit for your career.

Zip Recruiter is another site that can show you a lot of different opportunities. Their claim to fame is that they have over nine million jobs posted at any given time. Keep in mind that there are jobs posted all over the world, in different cities, and in different markets. They do a great job of breaking down the jobs by location, function, industry, and currently trending. When you upload your resume or type in your title and location, Zip Recruiter pulls up a lot of jobs related to your job search. It gives you a lot of options, but you must be very selective about which ones are really a good fit for you. Zip Recruiter can sometimes give too much information, but it's a good resource that will help you develop many options and opportunities.

Monster and Career Builder have been around for a long time now. These sites are a great place to search for corporate jobs but not the best place for small company jobs. Monster was once the leader in job postings, but other sites now post more jobs, including Indeed. Monster and Career Builder are good sites on which to post your resume because a lot of hiring managers and recruiters will see it. Remember, the more visible your resume is online, the better chances you'll be contacted about a job opportunity that might interest you.

You are your own brand in your job search efforts. It is imperative to have a specific and consistent message in your career search efforts in both social media and in your resume. Many career seekers are not consistent in their message about who they are, what they do, what their skills are, and what value they bring to an organization. If you have a specific message about leadership abilities on one major platform (i.e. LinkedIN) you must have that same consistent message on OTHER social media platforms AND on your resume. This will help you brand yourself in a way that shows the hiring authorities your true value and skills set that you can bring to their company. If you find that one message isn't working for you consistently, then it might be time to change that message. The key here is that you stay consistent in your message and in your own brand when presenting yourself in your job search.

Being in a specific market segment in your career can be advantageous for your job search. For example, if you know you've spent the majority of your career in the manufacturing and packaging markets, you have a huge a huge advantage. In these markets, you are exposed to a huge supply chain of materials, manufacturers, converters, end users, and consultants, and if you want to stay in the same market segment you've been in, they will likely be the first targets in your search for the position you want to pursue. It's also likely you know some of your competitors. Search for jobs with those competitors. They will see you as having the most value to bring to their organization.

If you have a non-compete with your previous or current employer, please do take that into serious consideration. Legal problems with non-compete agreements will be a hindrance, but there are sometimes ways around them. For all intents and purposes, it's best to find and identify an attorney who specializes in non-compete agreements. You don't have to contact one right away, but identifying a few will help you in the future if you interview with a competitor.

There are exceptions to signed non-compete and nondisclosure agreements. You will want to start by researching whether your state is a "right to work" state. That means a non-compete will likely be very easy to work around in the legal process. Attorneys know the most about these matters, but it's more likely that you will be able to pursue and accept a job with a competitor in a "right to work" state than in a state where non-compete or nondisclosure agreements hold up in a court of law. Some considerations to think about are the dates on your agreement, where you signed the non-compete, and where the company headquarters is located.

Employment laws change from year to year in different states and countries. For research purposes, please check this website to see if your state is a right to work state.

https://nrtwc.org/facts-issues/state-right-to-work-timeline-2016/

This site will provide more information, and you will be able to see if you can pursue a competitor based on your state's right to work laws. If you have any major concerns about your agreement, it's surely worth your time to consult an attorney who specializes in right to work, non-compete, and nondisclosure laws. Obviously, if you did not sign a non-compete or a nondisclosure contract, you needn't worry about this step in the process.

There are some additional things you should be aware of. If you do have a non-compete or nondisclosure, and the company fires you or lets you go as a part of a company layoff, your current signed agreement will be null and void. The only exception to that rule is if you are offered a severance payment. If the company offers you a severance, they will likely have you sign another document. When you sign that severance document, it is highly likely that you will be subjected to a further non-compete or nondisclosure contract that will extend past the severance payment date. Severance always seems like a good idea *until* you realize you are bound by a non-compete or nondisclosure contract as part of the severance. That can be difficult to navigate around when starting to search for another job, so please keep that in mind when signing a severance agreement.

Now that you've figured out whether you can pursue a competitor, you can begin searching for your new position by researching your competitors' openings. Often, they will post them online. You don't want to apply for these jobs online immediately. The online application process is a "black hole" for candidates. It's not enough to apply online for a job you're considering. It's a better tactic to do more research to find the hiring manager for these positions. Applying online can be your last-ditch effort, but it shouldn't be your starting point. Doing the research to find out what jobs are available is the best starting point.

When you research your next job opportunity, start by doing some digging and considering the *whole* supply chain of the products, services, or offerings you are involved with at your current company. In packaging and manufacturing markets, the supply chain starts with the chemicals, polymers, and raw materials companies in which your products are manufactured. It's a great first practice to list the entire supply chain—from raw material to manufacturer to converter to end user.

For example, if you are a manufacturer of packaging products, make a list of the supply chain as it relates to your manufactured product. A general example is below:

➢ Chemicals, Inks, Coatings

➢ Paper and Pulp Manufacturers

➢ Machine/Capital Equipment Manufacturers

➢ Packaging Manufacturer (your company)

➢ Converters

➢ Printers

➢ Distributors

➢ Specialist Recruiters

➢ End Users

Now that you've listed the whole supply chain, it's time to do more research. The best way to research is to find the industry associations at each stage of the supply chain. Identify the top industry association and then find a list of suppliers of the raw materials your company uses in its manufacturing process.

For example, if you make packaging products, the first step in the supply chain is the pulp and paper manufacturer and the chemical companies that manufacture the additives, coatings, and chemicals that go into pulp and paper manufacturing. Find the industry association most relevant to the materials your company uses (in this case, it's TAPPI, Technical Association of Paper and Pulp Industry, www.tappi.org) and research the companies that manufacture that material. A good place to look for these industry associations is in either the Buyer's Guide or Member Directory.

Once you find the companies that manufacture the material in an industry list, go to each company website to see if they have specific openings listed online. If they do, write down the openings and make a list of the ones you want to apply for. This master list will serve as a reference point as you research to find the decision makers you can contact to apply for the position.

Once you've identified the supply chain and have researched the industry association in that segment of the supply chain, I would recommend going to the next step in your supply chain list and repeating the exercise by researching, identifying, and listing all the companies that have opportunities you may want to pursue. Make your way through the supply chain of your current company, stopping at the end user. This will help you figure out which opportunities seem most viable and interesting to you. You can rank them and begin pursuing the opportunities you are most interested in first.

Another great way to find new job opportunities is to find them through your previous skills set. Many of us are trained in a specific software program, quality control method (i.e. ISO 9001), or regulatory standards. It's crucial to identify those unique skills and qualifications prior to searching for your new position. Once you've identified those skills, search for jobs via those specific skills. Typing the skills or experiences you've had into the job search engines you use online will prove to be a very good way to source opportunities that you will be qualified for at the next job in your career. This is a creative way to find new jobs to apply for if you are having difficulty finding a job that you want. Try this the next time you get stuck in your job search, and perhaps it will open some doors for you to apply for more opportunities.

Now that you've identified the opportunities you want to pursue, the next step is to research—online or through industry connections in your network—the potential hiring managers. Under each opportunity, make a list of the potential hiring managers, their titles, and their locations. The next step is to figure out their phone numbers and email addresses. Sometimes this information can be found online, and sometimes not. Google can be your greatest asset, but you can also find this information in online business directories. Some of these are free, and some are not. If there is a fee to use them, evaluate how valuable the information is to you. If you are serious about the next stage in your career, it will be money well spent. Your return on investment will be huge, and there is nothing better than investing in yourself and your career.

"Opportunities don't often come along. So, when they do, you have to grab them."
– Audrey Hepburn

The next step in your search is to call the hiring manager directly to talk (or leave a message) about opportunities with the company. You will want to write up a general script (but don't read it when you call them) and practice the call ahead of time. Plan to have a few specific points about your qualifications and your interest in the position to discuss. The goal of this call is to get a specific job description and find out if you can send your custom resume directly or if you must go through human resources. The ideal situation is sending it to them directly so you will be considered for the position. If you must go through human resources, don't argue—just follow directions. The fact that you've already called or emailed about the opportunity is strong enough evidence, in their eyes, that you are serious about the position and want to move forward to pursue the opportunity.

Another great place to start is with a recruiter that specializes in your specific market segments. Recruiters have a pulse on the opportunities out there in the market. Often, companies go directly to the recruiter for help in hiring the best possible candidate for each specific role they have open. If you are starting your search, it never hurts to contact a specialist recruiter who has credentials, long-term experience, and exposure to the markets.

Before you send a resume or cover letter to the hiring manager or human resources person, you will want to customize them. This is an important step because a generic resume will not attract as much interest from the hiring authorities as a custom one will. The way you customize the resume and cover letter is to identify the key words, functions, responsibilities, and details of the role and position and use that information to add details to your resume. Don't embellish your experience, and don't include any information in your custom resume or cover letter that you don't have experience with. It won't help you during the interview process because the hiring manager will be asking you for more details about your experience and knowledge. Remember, their focus is to find someone who has specific skills that will help them in their business. Building trust, integrity, and rapport with the hiring managers and interviewers is crucial to landing the job you want.

Do the same with your five top-ranked opportunities, contacting the hiring manager or human resource manager via your custom resume. If you wish, you can follow the same process with the remaining opportunities as well. It's a numbers game, and finding the best possible opportunity involves getting different companies to pursue your candidacy for their specific opening. When you have more than one company interested in you, you will have more leverage when seriously considering opportunities and offers.

I'm sure you will be eager to move forward to the interview process, but most candidates don't understand that there will be a considerable time lag between when they apply and when the company chooses to interview. Sometimes the first contact from the company will take a week, and sometimes it will take a few months. The most important next step is to follow up with the employer and hiring authorities.

As a general rule, you'll want to follow up about a week to ten business days after you send your resume. If you leave a message and they don't respond, don't panic. Try them again in another week to ten days. One very important rule is to listen very closely to what they say to you when you follow up. If they tell you it will take another few weeks, don't call in a week. In that case, call them in two weeks. Don't follow through too early because you will be seen as being too eager and impatient. Those are not qualities you want to be perceived as having.

If the company does not respond after following up three times, it's best to move on to the next opportunity. You don't want to pursue an opportunity with a company that doesn't have an interest in moving forward with you. You usually won't know why they aren't interested. Just keep in mind that there could be a whole slew of reasons they aren't moving forward. Here are just some of the reasons the company may not have gotten back to you:

1. They aren't ready to start the interview process.

2. Something has changed internally within the company.

3. The hiring manager is on vacation or holiday.

4. They are busy with their current business and customers and don't have time now.

5. They are traveling on business or to trade shows.

6. They are pursuing other candidates.

7. They don't think you are the ideal candidate for their position.

8. They are considering someone they perceived as a more "perfect" fit for the role.

9. They are talking to people who know you and have worked with you in the past.

10. They are waiting for their team to get back to them with their feedback.

11. They think you are the ideal candidate, but they want to find another potential candidate to whom they can compare your background.

The important part is to be patient. You don't know the reasons why they aren't getting back to you, and you can't possibly guess what their situation is and at what stage they are in the hiring process. Follow up with them about three times, and if it doesn't move forward, then let it go. If they do identify you as someone they want to move forward with in their process and choose to get back to you, the timing and details of their reasoning will likely come to light in the interview process. At that point, you'll be on your way.

Chapter 6

The Interview Process

"We all prospect, and don't even know we're doing it. When you start the dating process, you are actually prospecting for the person you want to marry. When you're interviewing employees, you are prospecting for someone who will best fit your needs."
– Zig Ziglar

Part 1: Stepping into the Interview Process

When a company decides they want to interview for a position, there are probably going to be several steps. The interview process is the most important stage in securing the job you desire. There are a lot of variables and things to consider when interviewing, and you should be aware of the many things that can happen. Every company follows a different process, and sometimes the interview processes within a single company can vary. The most important thing in the interview process is being prepared and presenting yourself well to your interviewers.

The first step involved with the interview process is a request for an interview. When the hiring company or hiring authority contacts you, ask them kindly what the process will entail. Often, they will start with a phone interview and progress to face-to-face interviews with the hiring managers and their team. The reason you'll want to find out beforehand is to make sure you are prepared and ready for each step in the process.

A phone interview can be a challenging stage because many candidates don't prepare for it or know how to sell their qualifications to the person on the other end of the phone. If a hiring manager requests a phone interview, you'll want to prepare as much as possible. Your ultimate goal is to sit down with the company face to face, but to be invited for a face-to-face interview, you'll need to properly prepare so that you can sell yourself and impress the hiring manager in the phone interview.

Because you're going to have to sell yourself over the phone, being comfortable on the phone is key. Set time aside to prepare. Review the formal job description again. Look at the details, and then look at the custom resume you presented to the company at the application stage and make sure you are ready to talk about your experience. Research the role you are applying for at the company and do some research about the company's products and markets. You must be absolutely prepared to talk about how you are the best possible fit for the position. Often, a single question by the hiring manager that is not answered correctly can prevent a candidate from being asked for a face-to-face interview.

One of the most important things to remember for an interview is to be your true self. If you are prepared for the questions before they happen, you will feel more comfortable, and that will help you to be authentic in your answers. You should always expect to be asked a question you haven't prepared for. Being yourself and being authentic will help you maintain your composure.

> "My interviewing style and my approach to things is that, yes, it's okay to be sincere; it's okay to be yourself; it's okay to be real."
> – Eddie Trunk

One advantage you have during the phone interview stage is that the hiring manager on the other line of the phone cannot see you (unless it's a video conference call). In your preparation for the phone interview, write down some questions you have about the opportunity on a piece of paper. At some point in the conversation with the hiring manager, it will benefit you to bring up some of these questions. However, be sure that when you ask these questions, you ask them in the *flow* of the conversation and that they are a natural progression in your conversation. This is key. For example, don't just start asking questions about compensation, benefits, vacation, or how you get paid at the company before you've even had a chance to explain to the hiring manager why you are the best possible fit for the opportunity.

Having questions prepared and written down, and keeping them in view when you are being interviewed over the phone, will help you decide *when* you are going to bring them up. It's quite possible you won't get to ask these questions, but that's okay. You want to let the hiring manager lead the conversation. Be polite, and don't interrupt or insert your thoughts, ideas, or concerns while the interviewer is talking.

Answer the interviewer's questions succinctly, short and to the point. If you answer a question, and it seems natural to ask one of your questions at the end of your answer, you can do so. Just be cautious and always allow the interviewer to lead the conversation.

Because the main goal is to secure a face-to-face interview, the last key component in the conversation is to ask to meet the hiring authorities and their team, or at least suggest it. Most great salespeople know that you must ask for the order. Interviewing is very similar to sales because you are selling yourself. At the end of the conversation, you might ask, "What are the next steps in the interview process?" You should mention that you look forward to meeting the team or that you're interested in proceeding with the interview process. This is called *closing*. You need to show the company you know how to sell yourself because that is a direct reflection of how well you will be able to sell their products and represent the company properly when working with customers, colleagues, competitors, distributors, consultants, and the company's business partners.

When you are fortunate enough to be invited for a face-to-face interview, you will again want to be as prepared as possible. I've experienced a lot of strange, abstract, and destructive tendencies during the interview stage with candidates I've worked with over the years. Preparation will prevent this from happening and will allow you to present yourself in the best light possible.

The first step is deciding on the interview date. When a hiring authority asks you for an interview, you are wise to accept the dates they ask you to meet with them. If your schedule does not permit because of another business appointment, it is acceptable to let them know you have another business meeting in your schedule. If you have a personal appointment during the requested time to interview, it would be wise to clear your schedule and cancel or reschedule your personal appointment unless it's health-related. If it is health-related, take caution in how you share this, but make sure the company understands it's a medical issue. The company isn't permitted to discriminate against health-related matters in their interview process, but let's face it, companies will do whatever they want when considering a candidate they want to hire. I've never specifically seen discrimination from any company I've worked with, but I do know that you don't want to portray yourself as someone who is difficult to work with, or you run the risk of not landing the job. Do your best to clear your schedule and make time for the face-to-face interview when they request it.

During this time, ask important details you will need to know for the face-to-face interview. Find out the exact time and time zone for the interview request. You also need to know the location and directions on where to park, the specific location within the company building, the person you will be meeting with in the interview (or the names of the interview team), who to ask for, and what type of attire you should wear. If the company doesn't give you specifics on clothing, always err on the side of caution and dress as nicely as possible. Nowadays, there is a trend toward business casual without a tie. This trend might last for a long time, but it's better to be safe than sorry during your interviews.

"Better three hours too soon than a minute too late."
– William Shakespeare

When you agree to an interview, don't show up late! If you are tardy or late to the phone or face-to-face interview, you will already have one strike against you regardless of the circumstance. When you show up late to the interview, the hiring managers will immediately be thinking to themselves, "Will this person show up late to work? To meetings with our customers or clients? To meetings in the office? To important events?" By showing up late, you show the interviewers you aren't serious about your career or about being the best you can be every day.

"When interviewing for any job, you of course want to dress appropriately for the position, but you also want to stay true to who you are."
– Nina Garcia

Just like you mother told you, first impressions *do* mean a lot to people. How you present yourself in the face-to-face interview is very important. That means you should be both clean and clean-shaven, your hair should look as good as possible, and you should wear matching clothes, shoes, and accessories. It also means you should smile during your interview, but be sure there is a balance. Smile at appropriate times when you meet someone or part ways with someone during the interview. Don't smile when you are asked a very serious question or when talking about a difficult, painful, depressing, or bad subject. Be conscious, and be in the moment. Act natural and be yourself. Look the hiring managers and their team in the eye when answering their questions because it shows you are focused and not afraid of being authentic. This is the best advice I have for candidates during the face-to-face interview process.

Another important element of the face-to-face interview is the resume. Be sure to bring at least a few copies of your current and updated custom resume. The resume you bring to the interview needs to be exactly the same as the one you originally sent with your cover letter during the application process. Don't alter it, change it, or make any adjustments during this stage in the interview process. You typically meet only with the people you were asked to meet during the face-to-face interview, but be prepared with extra copies of your resume just in case. Make sure your resume is neat, organized, and presented as well as possible. If you wish to bring a folder to put the resume copies into, you can. I would also bring a pen and an extra piece of paper in case you wish to take some notes during the interview. It's not mandatory, but it shows your preparedness.

Candidates often get so nervous and caught up in the interview process that they are their own worst enemies. Being prepared will help you in the interview. Study the questions you have written down. Stand in front of a mirror to practice your answers to questions you *know* they will ask you. If you have family or friends to practice with, ask them to help you by asking you random questions about the job. This will help prepare you to ad lib or improvise your answers. If you have a problem with sweating when you are nervous, being prepared will help you to remain calm and not sweat profusely during the face-to-face interview. Don't overthink this meeting. Just do your best and know that the preparation you put into it will have set you up for success when the time comes to meet everyone you wish to work with in your new job.

Don't drink three cups of coffee before you arrive on the day of the interview, or you'll run the risk of being nervous, sweating, or acting out of character. In other words, maintain your normal routine prior to the interview. If you exercise, do so early in the day. If you meditate or do yoga, do that before you arrive to maintain your energy levels but also to remain calm.

When you get to the interview, be, act, and present yourself as naturally as possible. Of course you're excited, but you must manage that energy and excitement. Therefore, proper preparation and maintaining a normal life schedule beforehand is very important. When you meet the hiring managers, shake their hands, but don't squeeze too tight, hold on forever, or have a limp handshake. Just shake firmly and let go after one second. Look the hiring managers and their team in the eye when answering their questions to show your focus and authenticity.

During the interview, the company and its representatives will surely ask you why you're considering this new career opportunity. Be prepared for this question. Answer it as diplomatically as you can. Don't ramble on about your current or previous employer, saying a lot of negative things about them, and don't act bitter. Be prepared to answer this question in a nice way without sounding rude, angry, upset, or sad about your experience with them. I advise you to let the hiring manager know that you're just looking for the next challenge in your career, and you are excited about the opportunity to grow with a new company. If they press you on this topic, explain that the past is the past, you have no sour grapes, you learned a lot from your experience at your previous place of employment, and you're ready to grow into a new opportunity. They will be forced to accept this answer. Do not give them any details, and if they ask, let them know again that you are thankful to have had the experience with your former company and want to focus on the positives.

Compensation is a touchy topic, and it's a crucial step in gaining the interviewer's trust and confidence that you will be completely transparent and a good communicator on their team if the company chooses to hire you. Take caution and be sure you are completely comfortable with this topic. If you are not, you can tell them you are not comfortable discussing it, but it's likely to be in your best interest to have this discussion.

If the interview team asks you about your current compensation figures, be as open and honest with them about it as you can. If they don't ask about compensation, do not bring it up to them. It will likely be discussed at a later time if you get to the offer stage. Prepare for this question, though, because if they ask you about it, it's an important part of their process. If you filled out an online application in the past and listed your compensation on the application form, make sure you are consistent with that figure.

If you make more with your current company than the new company is offering for the position, realize that most companies do have some flexibility, within reason, on compensation. Also, take into consideration that being happy at a company, in a role you like, with an opportunity for career advancement may be more important than a specific dollar figure. This is also the time to ask the interviewer about any relevant questions regarding compensation, sales commissions, benefits, vacation, car allowance or company vehicle benefits, 401k/retirement, profit sharing, and the opportunity for advancement in the future. All of these topics are very important, and you must take all variables into account.

Part 2 Interview Do's and Don'ts

Do:

➤ Research the company before the interviews.

➤ Prepare for the interview by writing down questions you know you will be asked.

➤ Prepare by answering questions in front of a mirror or with family or friends.

➤ Study your questions and answers before the interview.

➤ Stay calm during all stages of the interview process.

The Interview Process

➤ Maintain a normal day's routine before the interview.

➤ Ask for face-to-face interview details beforehand (time, place, who you'll meet with).

➤ Dress as well as possible.

➤ Bring extra copies of your resume.

➤ Bring a pen and paper just in case.

➤ Properly groom yourself.

➤ Smile when meeting, greeting, or departing from the interview team members.

➤ Ask the next steps at the end of the interview.

➤ During the phone interview, have your questions in front of you.

➤ During the face-to-face interview, study and remember the important questions you have.

➤ Be honest.

➤ Ask questions you have *only* in the natural flow of conversation.

➤ When being asked for an interview, do your best to accommodate the dates and times the interviewer wants to talk with you or meet you.

➤ Shake hands naturally and firmly and not too long or too soft.

➤ Ask for the job or imply you are the best person for the job they are interviewing you for.

- Stay focused.

- Answer questions directly and to the point with short answers when needed.

- Have an answer ready when they ask you why you're considering leaving your current employer or why you are no longer with your current employer.

- Ask for business cards from the interview team.

- Be natural.

- Be *authentic!*

- Answer questions about compensation directly.

Don't:

- Reschedule the interview unless there is an emergency.

- Ask questions out of the context of the conversation.

- Shake hands too hard, too soft, or too long.

- Wear clothes that don't match or are not appropriate business attire.

- Show up ungroomed.

- Show up unprepared.

- Drink too much coffee.

- Eat too much before the meeting.

The Interview Process

- ➤ Show up sick or ill to the interview.

- ➤ Interrupt the interviewers.

- ➤ Sweat profusely.

- ➤ Fidget, tap your hands or feet, or shake your legs.

- ➤ Be nervous or portray yourself as nervous to the interview team.

- ➤ Show up late to the interview.

- ➤ Show up to the interview without your current custom resume and cover letter.

- ➤ Change your resume or cover letter before the interview.

- ➤ Give the hiring manager reason to be concerned about you in any way.

- ➤ Abruptly leave the interview.

- ➤ Speak out of turn.

- ➤ Leave without finding out what the next steps are or when you'll hear from them.

- ➤ Press them to give you an answer.

- ➤ Be in a hurry to leave the interview.

- ➤ Be negative or focus on negatives in the interview process.

- ➤ Talk negatively about your employer.

- ➤ Drink alcohol, do drugs, or show up drunk to the interview.

> ➢ Leave the interview without asking for the business cards of the interview team.

> ➢ Let compensation be the only defining factor in making the decision to move forward or not.

Part 3 Proper Interview Follow-Up

"Follow up the interview with a phone call. If Carrot Top can figure out how to use a phone, so can you."
– Tom Cole

During your interview, listen very closely to what the interviewers tell you about their process after a face-to-face interview and when they will make a decision. They will likely make it clear when you should be hearing from them. If they don't, be as patient as possible after the interview.

After your face-to-face interview, you will likely be eager to know the opinions and feedback from the hiring managers. If you got their business cards, you have the information you need to get this information. Remember that there is a fine line between not following up quickly enough and following up too quickly. Based on my experience, I believe you should wait until the next day to follow up, regardless of the business day.

You'll want to allow time for the interviewers to discuss the interviews. There might have been one or two things they discussed briefly immediately after the interviews, but they likely won't have made a decision. Even if they have already decided whether or not to move forward with you to the next stage in the hiring process, they may take a few days to get back to you. Remember that they have busy schedules. The interview is important to their company, but their priority is always their current responsibilities—working with customers, products, or processes that are crucial to their business's success.

Once again, the most professional thing you can do is to send them an email one day after the interviews. I wouldn't expect an immediate response. Give the company a few days to get back to you. If they respond within a day or two, that is a positive development. After you have followed up with them a day after the interview, you will want to wait seven to ten business days before you follow up again. It's very likely that by this point they will have already gotten back to you. Most job searches have an urgency, and they get back to the candidate quickly because they want to hire for the position. If it's been about seven to ten business days before you hear back from them, there is a likelihood that they are not interested in moving forward. Either way, you have done your best, and you know you have put your best foot forward. Be ready to let the chips fall as they may.

You Got The Job!

Here is a sample follow-up email you can customize for your own needs:

Attn: Name

Company

Street

City, State Zip

Dear _____,

Thank you for the interview on _____. I enjoyed meeting you and learning about the Operations position available with _____. I see vast opportunities for your products and services in the _____ territory.

My experience with the manufacturing of _____ will provide a solid foundation for the successful sales of your entire product line. The energy I invest in customer-oriented sales and service would be a perfect fit with your organization. Networking relationships I have developed with past customers and suppliers in multiple industries in the _____territory will be to our mutual benefit.

I look forward to meeting with you soon to pursue this position. I am confident I can develop and implement a sales plan that will address _____ targeted goals. As a team player, I will contribute immediately to the success of _____.

Sincerely,

Your Name

If you are working with an outside recruiter, the recruiter will be able to follow up on your behalf as well. Contact the recruiter after the interview to discuss the interview details. Ask him if he has heard anything about the face-to-face interview yet. If not, ask him to kindly follow up with the company within five business days to find out if they have any feedback from the interview for you. This way, the recruiter will follow up, and it won't seem as though you are too eager.

Lastly, be patient. I've seen companies make an offer during an interview, and I've also seen companies wait over a month to make an offer. The latter is a very rare case, but it has happened, and there is usually a good reason for it. Often, around the holidays and employee vacations, companies take a long time to provide feedback. Understand that there a lot of factors, and know that, in due time, you will either be continuing your job search or on your way to the offer stage. Hopefully, the company has gotten back to you and has mentioned they will be in touch with the next stage of the interview process. The best-case scenario is an offer.

Chapter 7

Job Offer Stage

Without a doubt, the most exciting part of the whole hiring process is the job offer stage. Although it's invigorating and thrilling to be selected, it's important to take great care in this part of the hiring process.

In the ancient Chinese book, the *Tao Te Ching*, a section of Chapter 64 states,

> "People usually fail when they are on the verge of success. So give as much care to the end as to the beginning; Then there will be no failure."
> – Lao Tzu

This highlights the importance of taking as much care in the offer stage as you take in the rest of the hiring stages. It's crucial to choose your words carefully to ensure you don't misstep or misspeak.

If you played your cards right during the application and interview processes, you've already established your current compensation and your desired compensation with the hiring managers. In this case, there shouldn't be any surprises when they make an offer. If you have not given them numbers, I advise you to try to find out from the job description what the compensation is so you can position yourself for their offer. If they don't ask you what you make, be prepared for them to throw out a random number, and that, unfortunately, means a low offer. If that's the case, don't get discouraged. If you continue to play your cards right, all is not lost.

In most cases, you'll be made aware that an offer is coming. Hopefully, they do tell you that you will be getting an offer, and then you can figure out how to respond. They will likely be making a verbal offer first. It's my advice that you respond honestly. Don't lead them on and ask for it in writing unless you are serious about the figures and compensation they are offering. If they don't tell you the compensation figures, it's anyone's guess how it will look on paper.

Verbal offer or not, it's *always* crucial to ask for the offer in writing. You must see the full package and have time to understand it before deciding if it's something you can accept. Often, the base salary compensation will have sounded good on the phone, but after evaluating it on paper versus your current compensation and benefits or what you were expecting to see, it doesn't always end up being equal.

It's important to *know* what you are willing to accept before you even get the offer. Therefore, it's important to list all your current or previous compensation figures so you can determine how the two compare and whether you are going to accept or not. Here is a worksheet to determine current or previous compensation:

BENEFITS CHECKLIST

○   Base Salary

_____

○   Bonus & Commission

_____

○   Company Car or Allowance

_____

○   Vacation

_____

○   Life Insurance

_____

○   Disability

_____

○   Medical Insurance

_____

○   Dental/ Eyewear

_____

○   Profit Share or Stock Options

_____

Job Offer Stage

O   401K or Pension

_____

O   Relocation Expenses Expected

_____

O   Physical Moving Expense/Household Goods

_____

O   Temporary Living Expense

_____

O   House Hunting Trips

_____

O   Closing Costs, Bank & Real Estate Fees

_____

O   Special Relocation Expense

_____

O   Additional Information

_____

It's important to fill this out before the offer stage. In doing so, you will be ready to compare it to whatever offer you receive.

Assuming you now have the offer in writing, I suggest you go over it with a fine-tooth comb. This means you should look it over carefully and compare every detail to your current or previous compensation. If it looks acceptable, I do *not* advise counteroffering. There is no point in playing games, trying to get more money from the company, or pushing them to the edge because then you risk losing the job opportunity you want so badly.

If there are discrepancies, however, your only course of action is to present a counteroffer. I caution you that this is a *very* touchy subject, and you should *only* present a counteroffer if there is no possible way you can accept what they have presented. Even though you might have some leverage over the company because you know they need you or want you on their team, it's still best to present a counteroffer *only* if you are sure their offer doesn't match your expectations.

If you do present a counteroffer, put it in the form of a question rather than a demand or necessity. It's always best to *ask* for a possible change or to *suggest* that all parts of your former/current company's compensation and the new company's package are not equal. For example, if everything in the offer looks great, but the company is only offering two weeks of vacation time, whereas you currently receive four weeks, it's best to let them know. Follow up their offer immediately by *asking*, "Is there anything we can do about that?" or "Is there any flexibility in that part of the offer?" By asking them, you show them that you are diplomatic, easy to work with, fair, and not pushy or demanding. If they say "No, we cannot change the vacation days in your offer," then you have a serious decision to make. Is it worth passing on the offer? Could you come back with something like "Is there a way to make things more equal in another part of the offer?" You should only try this approach, however, if you expect to decline the offer as it is and are serious about substituting another benefit for what you're giving up.

Assuming you work out the compensation details, you are on your way to reviewing the new final offer in writing. If all things are as they should be, you should send the company an email with an offer acceptance and sign and return the offer. Below is a sample offer acceptance letter you can customize and send to your new company.

Sample Acceptance Letter:

(Date)

(Employer)

(Company Name)

(Address)

(City, State, Zip)

Dear (Employer Name):

I am happy to accept your offer as defined in your letter dated (letter date here) for the position of (position) with your company. My understanding is that I will receive an annual salary of ($ amount). I will be able to start work with your firm on (start date).

Thank you very much for the opportunity to work with you and (company). Between now and my start day, you can reach me at the phone numbers below or contact me through (my recruiter here). I look forward to a long and productive career with (employer name).

Sincerely,

(Your name)

Home phone xxx xxx xxxx

Work phone xxx xxx xxxx

Other phone xxx xxx xxxx

Recruiter phone xxx xxx xxxx

Job Offer Stage

Upon returning the final signed offer, it's best to send a thank-you email or letter to the hiring manager with whom you negotiated the offer. It's important to start building trust, communication, and a positive working relationship with your new coworkers and colleagues. Showing respect, graciousness, and thankfulness is a sign to the new team that you are going to work well with them now and in the future. This job offer is laying the foundation for the start of your new career with the new company, and it's important to start off on the right foot. If you follow these instructions, you'll be on your way to making this the best job you've ever accepted.

Chapter 8

How to Leave Your Current Job

"Your work is to discover your work and then with all
your heart give yourself to it."
– Buddah

If you have a current job, there are many factors you must
consider in switching to a new position. If you are unem-
ployed, you won't have to worry as much about topics like
confidentiality, counteroffers, and leaving your current employer within a specific time frame. Therefore, you *might* be
able to skip over this chapter, but I still recommend reading it
through. It could prove to be extremely valuable for you in
the future. Being prepared for everything that comes with a
new job opportunity and possible counteroffer situation is
very important in the hiring process.

First and foremost, you are most likely going to want to
keep your new job search extremely confidential for obvious
reasons. There are some exceptions, like when there is "writing on the wall," as they say, at your current employer, but I
still advise keeping your career search quiet. You don't want
to lose your current position before you accept a new career
opportunity. Therefore, be cautious about telling anyone
about your search. Make it very clear to the hiring managers
and the team you are interviewing with that you would like to

keep things confidential because you don't want to sacrifice your current career and income. Usually, the human resources manager or recruiter is the person you can confide in to make sure the rest of the hiring team keeps your application and interest confidential and away from those outside of the company. You also want to maintain your reputation as someone who is loyal to their current career regardless of the reality that you're looking for a new career opportunity.

One rookie mistake you do not want to make is telling your current boss or employer that you are leaving the company *before* you have set a starting date with your new employer. I have seen many scenarios in which candidates accept a new position, let their current employer know they are leaving their current job, and then something unfortunate happens to nullify the signed offer letter from the new company. You must remember that after an offer is signed, you will likely be asked to complete a full background check, drug screen, and sometimes a physical.

During the background check, the new employer will confirm you do not have a felony record. They will look for legal problems with your city, state, or country. They will also be confirming the college degree on your resume. Sometimes the new employer will also confirm the work history on your resume by calling the previous companies you worked for. In rare cases, for positions working closely with company finances, they will check your outstanding debts and fiscal history.

One of the main reasons to be truthful on your application and resume is that the new employer will be double-checking everything before they allow you to work with them. They want to be sure you are being 100% truthful about your experience, education, and the dates on your resume.

Only after the new employer gets back to you with clearance on your background checks and drug checks should you give notice to your current employer. There are exceptions, but you typically don't want to risk losing your current career for a new one because being out of work without a paycheck can be devastating.

It's also important to leave on good terms with your current employer. You don't want to burn any bridges because you will likely run into them in the market, at trade shows, when you're with customers, or perhaps in your everyday life. It's standard practice to give your current employer at least two weeks of notice depending on the projects you currently have in place. Some employers will ask you to pack up your belongings and leave your job the same day. Some will ask you to finish the projects you've started with customers and coworkers. Always be kind and understanding when your current employer asks you to finish up projects.

The best way to let your employer know about your resignation is to talk with them about it face to face. If you can't talk to them face to face, you should talk to them on the phone. After letting them know about your resignation, I recommend sending a formal resignation letter.

The formal resignation letter or email is a standard practice with professionals. There are a lot of different scenarios for formal resignation letters, so you might want to draft a custom letter depending on your situation. How much information you offer them is up to you. You can find a lot of sample resignation letters online and customize them to your current situation. Below is a letter that can be modified to fit your specific and custom situation.

Sample Resignation Letter:

Date

Name

Company Name

Address

City, State Zip

Dear Mr. _____:

I have been presented with an exceptional opportunity with another organization, therefore I must resign my employment with _____, effective two weeks from today, _____ (date).

I have enjoyed the associations, friends, and the profitable relationship over my term of employment; however, my new opportunity will allow me to significantly expand my career. I wish the organization, my friends, and my associates success in their continued efforts.

Very truly yours,

Your Name

Once you've sent your resignation letter, you are on your way to leaving your current company. Your current employer may be disappointed by your departure and might try to keep you on the team by presenting you with a counteroffer. Counteroffers are a way for an employer to retain your skills, services, and employment with their company because they value your experience, but I must make something very clear to you. Under most circumstances, you should *never* accept a counteroffer from your current employer. This is a step toward career suicide. If and when you receive a counteroffer, think back to when you were looking for a new career opportunity.

➢ What were your motivations?

➢ What problems or situations did you have trouble with at your current job?

➢ Why did you decide you were going to look for a new job in the first place?

➢ Do you think that these problems, situations, or circumstances will change if you accept a counteroffer to stay with your current employer?

In almost all situations, you don't even want to consider this counteroffer. It's a way for your current employer to buy time, keep you on their team, and keep your expertise and experience around until the time when they can let you go. I've seen it countless times. Put yourself in your employer's shoes. If you have an employee who tried to leave your company, and you keep him or her on your team with a counteroffer, the moment there is a problem, the company has financial issues or goes through a downsizing period, or something negative happens within the company, you will want to let that employee go first because he already attempted to leave the company on his own.

I have compiled for you here some information, articles, and some questions and answers we send to our candidates when they are considering a counteroffer situation.

The Implications of a Counteroffer

A counteroffer can be very flattering, sometimes causing your emotions to obscure your objective decision to leave your present employer. There is also the natural feeling of "buyer's remorse," that vague apprehension of change that subtly urges you to reconsider your decision. When confronted with a counteroffer, ask yourself these questions:

1. I made a decision to leave because I felt another environment would better fulfill my career needs. If I stay, will the situation at my company really improve just because I said I was quitting?

2. If I decide to stay, will my loyalty be suspect and affect my chance for advancement in the future?

3. If my loyalty is in question, will I be an early layoff when business slows down?

4. They are offering me a raise to stay. Is it just my annual review coming early?

5. The raise they offered me is above their guidelines for my job. Does that mean they are just "buying time"

until they can find my replacement within their regular salary bracket?

6. In the final analysis, I got this counteroffer because I was going to resign. Will I have to threaten to quit every time I want to advance with my company in the future?

The Professional Approach

As a professional, you must make your career decisions objectively, free of the emotional pressures you are likely to feel later when being urged to reconsider. While well-meaning friends, relatives, and business associates will offer advice, you must depend primarily on your own judgment. After all, you are the only one who is in the position to understand all the implications of a counteroffer. Expect your company to be sorry to see you leave and to make some attempt to keep you. At best, their response should be considered flattering, but it is beset with pitfalls.

A counteroffer is really a belated affirmation of the contributions you have made to your old company. End your relationship with your employer as professionally as you began it. Your new company will be anxious to have you start, so you should do so as soon as possible. Two weeks' notice is usually sufficient.

Move ahead to your new job with the goal of making yourself as valuable to your new employer as you were to your old.

Is Your Job Any Better the Second Time Around?
by Joyce Lain Kennedy

Another company tempts you by offering more pay than you're currently earning. You tell your boss you're thinking of taking the job. But she says she'll match the offer and asks you to stay. What should you do?

The answer largely hinges on what value your boss places on you. Here's how two experts view "buybacks."

Counteroffers usually are counterproductive, observes Robert Kushell of Dunhill Personnel System in New York City. He says if your boss is keen to your level of expertise and growth objectives, and how much competitor's employees earn, she probably has been upgrading your responsibilities and pay to parity with the competition's, virtually eliminating the need to "buy" you back.

If that's not the case, says Kushell, and you're faced with choosing the greener pasture, you've got a problem that a counteroffer isn't likely to solve: Your present company isn't giving you the career recognition you feel you deserve. You're unappreciated where you are and are likely to remain so. Your inclination to leave may be viewed as disloyalty. If your boss gives you a raise and persuades you to stay, you can bet she's buying time to replace you—if you don't leave on your own first.

Q AND A

CAREERS

Get All Your Benefits When You Quit a Job
by Joyce Lain Kennedy

Dear Joyce: When I resigned last month from my previous position, I had five vacation days I didn't take. Should the company have paid me? If so, is it too late to collect? – L.Y.

A: Company policies vary on this question; query the human resources or personnel department where you formerly worked. If it was a tiny firm, ask your ex-boss. Nobody will be thrilled to hear from you about money owed, so begin by saying, "Because you've always been fair, I know you'll understand why I'm asking..." The next time you depart from a job, find out your organization's rules about severance, retirement, and health benefits. Here's a reminder checklist to save and use.

➤ Do you have severance pay coming? How much? Remember, severance money may or may not be paid when a company terminates you but almost never is paid when you voluntarily resign.

➤ Will you be compensated for accumulated vacation days? Accumulated sick days? Suppose a company's policy directs that you can be paid for up to thirty days of leave. Ask if you can take any excess days as time off before you quit.

➤ When do you get back any contribution you made to a retirement fund? Do you receive the accrued interest as well? Do you get all or any of your organization's contribution to a retirement fund?

➤ How long after resignation will your health and life insurance benefits remain in effect? New policies may have clauses like "pre-existing conditions." It may be worth it to continue coverage under your old policy as an individual. As examples, you might be pregnant and depend on health insurance to pay for the delivery, or you might have survived a bout with cancer and find you're not adequately covered by your new employer's policy for a year or so. Beyond looking after your financial interests, remember that you have nothing to lose by showing professional style in leaving.

➤ Tell your boss first, not your friends.

➤ Plan a brief but charming resignation speech to go along with your letter, one that emphasizes that while you're in a terrific place, you received an offer you couldn't refuse. Keep your resignation letter short, identifying your last day of work and repeating that you enjoyed your tenure.

➤ If you must fill out resignation forms or participate in an exit interview, don't reveal negative reasons for leaving. You may have to work with your former boss or coworkers in the future and may even want to re-join the organization at a later date.

➤ Sometimes you don't want current associates to know where you're going. In that case, simply write "unan-nounced" in the blank on the resignation form or tell the exit interviewer that you're not "ready to announce your new position."

– Reprinted from the National Business Employment Weekly

Counteroffer Acceptance

Road to Career Ruin

A Raise Won't Permanently Cushion Thorns in the Nest

by Paul Hawkinson

Matthew Henry, the 17th-century writer, said, "Many a dangerous temptation comes to us in fine gay colours that are but skin deep." The same can be said for counteroffers, those magnetic enticements designed to lure you back into the nest after you've decided it's time to fly away.

The litany of horror stories I have come across in my years as an executive recruiter, consultant, and publisher, provides a litmus test that clearly indicates counteroffers should never be accepted...EVER!

I define a counteroffer simply as an inducement from your current employer to get you to stay after you've announced your intention to take another job. We're not talking about those instances when you receive an offer but don't tell your boss. Nor are we discussing offers that you never intended to take, yet tell your employer about anyway as a "they-want-me-but-I'm-staying-with-you" ploy.

These are merely astute positioning tactics you may choose to use to reinforce your worth by letting your boss

116

know you have other options. Mention of a true counteroffer, however, carries an actual threat to quit.

Interviews with employers who make counteroffers, and employees who accept them, have shown that as tempting as they may be, acceptance may cause career suicide. During the past twenty years, I have seen only isolated incidents in which an accepted counteroffer has benefited the employee. Consider the problem in its proper perspective.

What really goes through a boss's mind when someone quits?

"This couldn't be happening at a worse time."

"This is one of my best people. If I let him quit now, it'll wreak havoc on the morale of the department."

"I've already got one opening in my department. I don't need another right now."

"This will probably screw up the entire vacation schedule."

"I'm working as hard as I can, and I don't need to do his work, too."

"If I lose another good employee, the company might decide to 'lose' me, too."

"My review is coming up, and this will make me look bad."

"Maybe I can keep him until I find a suitable replacement."

What will the boss say to keep you in the nest?

Some of these comments are common.

"During the past twenty years, I have seen only isolated incidents in which an accepted counteroffer has worked to the benefit of the employee."

"I'm really shocked. I thought you were as happy with us as we are with you. Let's discuss it before you make your final decision."

"Aw, gee, I've been meaning to tell you about the great plans we have for you, but it's been confidential until now."

"The VP has you in mind for some exciting and expanding responsibilities."

"Your raise was scheduled to go into effect next quarter, but we'll make it effective immediately."

"You're going to work for who?"

Let's face it. When someone quits, it's a direct reflection on the boss. Unless you're incompetent or a destructive thorn in his side, the boss might look bad by "allowing" you to go. His gut reaction is to do what has to be done to keep you from leaving until he's ready. That's human nature.

Unfortunately, it's also human nature to want to stay unless your work life is abject misery. Career changes, like all ventures into the unknown, are tough. That's why bosses know they can usually keep you around by pressing the right buttons.

Before you succumb to a tempting counteroffer, consider these universal truths:

Any situation in which an employee is forced to get an outside offer before the present employer will suggest a raise, promotion, or better working conditions is suspect.

No matter what the company says when making its counteroffer, you will always be considered a fidelity risk. Having once demonstrated your lack of loyalty (for whatever reason), you will lose your status as a "team player" and your place in the inner circle.

Counteroffers are usually nothing more than stall devices to give your employer time to replace you.

Your reasons for wanting to leave still exist. Conditions are just made a bit more tolerable in the short term because of the raise, promotion, or promises made to keep you.

Counteroffers are only made in response to a threat to quit. Will you have to solicit an offer and threaten to quit every time you deserve better working conditions?

Decent and well-managed companies don't make counteroffers...EVER! Their policies are fair and equitable. They will not be subjected to "counteroffer coercion" or what they perceive as blackmail.

If the urge to accept a counteroffer hits you, keep on cleaning out your desk as you count your blessings.

DOW JONES REPRINT SERVICE
P.O. Box 300
Princeton, New Jersey 08540
Published by the Wall Street Journal
Dow Jones and Co., Inc. 1983

Based on our countless experiences with candidates and coun-teroffers, I encourage you to say "no, thank you" if you are ever presented with a counteroffer from your current employ-er. It's a lesson learned the hard way for most employees. It's my goal to make sure you are happy long term in your new career, and accepting a counteroffer is a way to ensure this doesn't happen. I certainly don't want to hear about your nightmare situation with these scenarios. Therefore, please take heed of this value-added advice from experience.

Chapter 9

Your New Job

"Your work is going to fill a large part of your life, and
the only way to be truly satisfied is to do what you believe is great work. And the only way to do great work
is to love what you do. If you haven't found it yet,
keep looking. Don't settle. As with all matters of the
heart, you'll know when you find it."
– Steve Jobs

The final steps in your exciting new career position are a
relief, yet you may also be feeling a minuscule amount of
positive anxiousness. The relief comes from that fact that the
hard part is of your career search is finally over. The anxiousness comes from your innate desire to start off on the right
foot for the start date and onboarding process.

In all actuality, the final steps are clear. The human resources or hiring manager will set a specific start date on
which you will begin your new career. Oftentimes this will be
met with arranging details of the start date, the onboarding,
the work training, and the full introduction to your new team.
You've already developed some positive relationships with
your new company. Continue to build these relationships by
furthering your commitments to your promises. They say "a
man is only as good as his word." Therefore, when you say

you will do something in your onboarding process, make sure you do it in a timely and productive manner. This will ensure you grow your relationship and further the trust your team has for you.

The company will be watching you closely the first month or two to make sure you are fitting in well and fulfilling your commitments. They will likely be understanding of a few small mistakes, but don't be late to any meetings, don't cancel unless it's an absolute emergency, and don't fail to communicate important details during your onboarding process. Remember, real communication with your new company is key. Doing this ensures you're seen in a positive light so you can flourish, grow, and excel in your exciting new career!

Off you go! May your soar in success. All the best! Now and forever forward!

Dream Career Course

Finally, if you've enjoyed this book but feel like you may benefit from some amazing hands-on application and implementation, I can help. I've been helping professionals, like yourself, for over fifteen years by giving them hands-on training on how to get their dream job. I've built a proven system and hands-on online "Dream Career Course" that can help you take action and execute ALL of the teachings in this book. The "Dream Career Course" is packed with tons of information, applications, and action steps that will take you through a proven method to get the job you've always wanted. The best part is, you'll get the job as quickly as possible. In this field where I've helped thousands of people with this proven, step-by-step system, I've seen it, first hand, help make a massive difference in the lives of career professionals.

For a limited time, I'll be accepting new professionals into my "Dream Career Course."

If you sign up today, I'm offering some incredible bonuses that I've put together specifically for this course that will help you immediately. I've sold these bonus materials in the past for over $5,500 but if you sign up today, they're free to you when you take the course. Don't miss out on this opportunity to help catapult your career, get your dream job, and make more money!

Find me online at www.centralcandidates.com to sign up for the Dream Career Course that will help you transform your career.

Citations

Joyce Lain Kennedy, "Get All Your Benefits When You Quit a Job," *The Courier- Journal*, October 26, 1986.

P. Hawkinson, "Counter-Offer Acceptance Road to Career Ruin: A Raise Won't Permanently Cushion Thorns in the Nest," *The Wall Street Journal*, December 11, 1983.